This edition published in 1999 by
Gingko Press Inc.
5768 Paradise Drive, Suite J
Corte Madera, CA, 94925, USA
Telephone: +(415) 924 9615
Facsimile: +(415) 924 9608
Email: gingko@linex.com

First published in Australia in 1999 by
The Images Publishing Group Pty Ltd
ACN 059 734 431
6 Bastow Place Mulgrave Victoria 3170
Telephone: +(613) 9561 5544
Facsimile: +(613) 9561 4860
Email: books@images.com.au

©Copyright
The Images Publishing Group Pty Ltd 1999

Designed by Emery Vincent Design
Text by Jackie Cooper and Emery Vincent Design
Edited by Jackie Cooper and Julian Dahl
Film by Pageset Pty Ltd
Printed in Hong Kong

ISBN: 1-58423-032-0

Emery Vincent Design

ACKNOWLEDGEMENTS

For their
contributions
in the
development
of this
publication,
we thank:

Suzie Attiwill
Haig Beck
Jackie Cooper
Peter Steidl

Special thanks to
Tim Murphy,
Emery Vincent Design,
for his design and
production assistance

We also
acknowledge the
contributions
of the following
photographers:
James Cant
Craig Carlstrom
Earl Carter
Andrew Curtis
Scott Francis
John Gollings
Kate Gollings
Tim Griffiths
Trevor Mein
Graham Munroe
Willem Rethmeier

CONTENTS

A topography of typography

Suzie Attiwill

COLLECTION

This book is a space of collection: the collected works of Emery Vincent Design. Collected here are projects designed by the practice over the past two decades. They include two-, three- and four-dimensional works: invitations, magazines, catalogues, corporate identities, environmental graphics, videos, computer animations and wayfinding systems for cities. Also part of this collection are the people who have worked on the projects, texts written and given as lectures, snippets extracted from larger commentaries, as well as quotes from other, different voices. Collections entail a gathering together of what has already happened. They are in this sense museological acts. They offer a view of history as an assemblage of collected facts and objects which in their arrangement reflect as much on the present and its method of assembling as they do on the past. This same process is also apparent in culture. In a paper titled 'Australia: A culture of heterogeneity', Garry Emery speaks about Australian culture: 'it is based on collecting and then transforming elements from elsewhere…[We] Australians…understand that we are in the process of making culture, not just consolidating tradition. We are building something new, not repeating the past'. This book has been conceived of in the same way, as a collection that is about building something new, not so much about repeating and consolidating the past.

TEMPORAL

The work of Emery Vincent Design collected here is not gathered to present a retrospective of the practice. We have not endeavoured to be encyclopaedic in the collection process, and neither has there been an inventory-like approach to ordering the work. Nor has the book been produced in a spirit of nostalgia with a desire to collect the past so that it becomes tangible. Rather, the book is the product of Emery Vincent Design's active relation to the past, one where the value and usefulness of history in the present and to the future is continually recognised – a 'looking backwards to the future.' This is evident in the way the work is arranged. Instead of a linear chronological account of the practice from its beginnings, there are synchronic juxtapositions of time and content. Ideas and projects from different moments sit side by side. The conjunctions between form and content often produce dadaist effects. Ideas and techniques run as threads through different projects, disappearing and resurfacing in response to different client briefs. Projects completed a decade ago can still linger in the present, informing choices, offering ways of proceeding or rethinking, and providing continuity between the past and the future. The accidental too is important in the design process. This arrangement is like the design process itself, which is rarely a direct linear sequence.

PAUSE

To pause during the moving flow of things affects the act of gathering and collection. It provides an opportunity for critical distance and reflection on where one is at a given moment. This book is the product of such a pausing. Through pausing, what is present may be evaluated and collected. The pause allows the design practice to see and understand its work within contemporary contexts and culture. Pausing is valuable and timely at this moment of transition from one millennium into another. The book itself becomes a wayfinding device of this moment. A paused moment, a suspension in movement, is like the image on the cover – figures blurred, time delayed yet living. Both temporal and spatial, a moment full of movements of the past and the future becomes present. The image expresses this distilled moment in the history of the practice.

SPATIAL

A collection requires a taxonomy that is composed of categories into which things may be allocated. A taxonomy produces knowledge and a way of understanding what has been categorised. In this book, we did not want to establish stylistic or typological categories. We have attempted instead to find a way of working that does not so much interpret the projects, but which presents and communicates them directly. It became a question of finding a way that reflects how Emery Vincent Design operates and articulates the same processes of organising information. This book is itself another project concerned with the graphic presentation of information, so that readers can find their own paths through the work of the practice and navigate its history, philosophy and idiosyncrasies. An understanding of space is implicit throughout the work. Circulation, navigation and wayfinding are concerns at the core of Emery Vincent's design practice and philosophy – whether in two, three, or four dimensions. So it was logical to develop a system for the book that organises the information as a geographical taxonomy rather than alphabetically or typologically. This notion is easily understood in relation to three-dimensional space: space is represented in two dimensions in the form of maps which locate coordinates and significant landmarks. This gave us a key to make visible the spatial qualities implicit in the work and philosophy of Emery Vincent Design. It helped us to identify the markers and territory that the practice traverses. In reading this book, the reader is invited into this geography, to circulate and navigate around the work at will, to discover information through chance, desire, or curiosity, rather than as the result of a deterministic or didactic presentation of material. This book can be approached as an atlas of Emery Vincent Design, a mapping of its current topography – a topography of typography.

TOPOGRAPHY

A topography is defined as 'a detailed analysis and description of a region'. Here 'the region' is Emery Vincent Design. The analogy of mapping is extended in the process of collecting and organising the information in this book: lines of longitude and latitude provide a matrix. Longitude is derived from the Latin word meaning length. Meridians of longitude mark out differences in time: they locate things temporally. In relation to Emery Vincent Design, they represent the project 'lines'. Projects occur over time and they also mark time. Across these vertical lines that run from the top to the bottom of the page are the horizontal lines of latitude. This word comes from the Latin word meaning breadth. The breadth of the practice and its range of projects are mapped along these horizontal lines. They run like threads throughout the work of the past two decades. Nine lines of latitude are identified in this topography. The equatorial line through the middle is the line of Typography. Typography is central to everything that Emery Vincent Design does. On either side of this 'equator' are the other lines of latitude. This grid organises the presentation of work throughout the book. *Profile* This line at the top of the page locates the profile and history of the practice and the scope of work, including the type of projects, scale, and the various design disciplines involved. *Reference* This is a line for indicating the references, influences and homages to be discerned in particular projects. *Process* Along this latitude, the processes – technical, organisational – involved in the design of projects are described. *Philosophy* Close to the equator, this line locates Emery Vincent Design's philosophy and methodology. *Typography* The centre and core of the practice. *Place* This line identifies the spatial thread that runs through the work, and the transformation of space into place. *Identity* This is a line implicit in every project: design is about identity. *Modernism* Modernism has dominated the twentieth century. Emery Vincent Design negotiates and engages with modernism. This line locates the design practice within the broader realm of twentieth-century culture. *Graphics* A line at the base of every project. This is the grounding of the design practice. The lines of latitude occur through the entire book. They are always located in the same position, although they are not visible on every page. Readers may choose to orient themselves at any point by reference to this ordering matrix. Equally, it can be ignored.

GRID

The lines of longitude and latitude provide an implicit ordering device: an invisible grid is produced by their intersections and the formation of coordinates, locating material spatially on the page. This is both a mapping grid and a structural, graphic grid. The grid coordinates are determined variously by the material. If a conjunction between a project meridian and a line of latitude is significant, then the coordinate point is marked by a comment. Sometimes the grid is gently disrupted. In some ways the book resembles a puzzle. Depending on how different readers acknowledge or use the ordering devices, the book will be 'read' differently. This accords with the philosophy of Emery Vincent Design to simultaneously embrace rationalism and surrealism or chance conjunction as valid ways of ordering and understanding the world. Different ways of reading are therefore valid and encouraged. Readers are free to ramble through the book, to position themselves so that they can survey the work methodically, or discover haphazardly something of the practice. This book can be entered anywhere.

The primary choice of which way you organise something is made by deciding how you want it to be found

Richard Saul Wurman, *Information Architects*, Graphis Press Corp, Zurich, 1996, p17

As an ordering device in organising the presentation of the work

of Emery Vincent Design for publication,

we invoke the metaphor of the lines of longitude and latitude

that calibrate the globe. Here the meridians

of longitude equate with the temporal sequence of our projects,

while the lines of latitude correspond

to the nine threads that run through the work,

with typography, the central discipline

of the design practice, occupying the equatorial position

Profile

History of · Emery Vincent Design · Melbourne · Sydney · International · Project description · Design issues · Brief · Professional disciplines · Graphic designers · Corporate · identity strategist · Architects · Interior designers · New media designers · Marketing · Project management · Market research

Reference

Reference · Homage · Influence · Dada · Surrealism · Abstract expressionism · Magritte · Matisse · Picasso · Duchamp · Pollock · Brancusi · Bauhaus · De Stijl · Constructivism · El Lissitzky · Tadao Ando · Mies van der Rohe · Zwart · Minimalism · Zen · Popular culture · Calligraphy · Traditional printing · Poster art · Digital imagery

Process

Design process · Client · Analysis · Research · Brief writing · Collaboration · Intuition · Strategy · Technique · Structure · Tactics · Abstraction · Order/Chaos · Collage · Deconstruction · Layering · Chance · Conjunction · Fragmentation · Elegance · Harmony · Disruption · Hybridity · Information · Meaning · Persuasion · Space-time · Cyber

Philosophy

Critical distance · Existentialism · Rationalism · Empiricism · Pluralism · McLuhan

Typography

Word · Text · Type · Alphabet · Inscription · Palimpsest · Sign · Symbol · Emblem · Cipher · Function · Legibility · Clarity · Sense · Interpretation · Signification · Communication

Place

Context · Scale · Space · Light · Shadow · Time · Mood · Place making · Local memory · Genius loci · Urbanism · Public realm · Environmental graphics · Super graphics · Orientation · Wayfinding · Legibility · Tactility · Materiality · Phenomenology

Identity

Local · Regional · Global · Corporate · Memorable · Visual identity · Logo · Sign · Trademark · Branding · Livery · Definition · Image

Modernism

Avant garde · Purist · Minimalist · Classic · Surreal · Contemporary · Postmodern · Awards · Heterogeneity · Grid

Graphics

History · Theory · Technique · Technology · Digital

6   1

Jackie Cooper

Typography is
a fundamental thread
through our work

3

ABSENCE

Any designer will tell you, promoting design is an uphill grind. Who notices it? It's the absence of good design that impinges on people's awareness rather than its presence: badly designed things work inefficiently and feel uncomfortable to the body. But beyond such a basic threshold of awareness, people are generally unconcerned about design. It belongs to a rarefied world, not their ordinary everyday environment. Design resides somewhere remote alongside Style, the pair of them reserved for things that need to make a Statement of some kind. In the popular mind, design is associated with flamboyance, not with reserve or subtlety. The outrageous or unorthodox design gesture is seized on and either glorified or, more likely, ridiculed – a ritualised debunking that confirms and perpetuates the assumption of the uselessness of design. Or at the other extreme, design is perceived as austere and chilling, stripped of familiar embellishment: a confronting enigma.

INTEGRATION

In some societies, design exists undivided from other aspects of life. These tend to be homogeneous societies where a cultural thread connects people's lives, collective values and the production of artifacts. Shaker furniture, Japanese pottery, Scandinavian glassware, Italian fabrics and Balinese architecture are produced within traditions where design is unselfconsciously embedded in cultural expression, and where everyone is an artisan of some kind, a maker of things.

VANGUARD

Industrialisation, however, shattered the traditional mould of cultural value systems. Modernism launched a problematic cultural condition in which design became located in the 'vanguard' – by definition beyond the rest of society. Design leads and breaks new ground: it does not confirm or represent traditional social values. This cleavage between design and modern society explains a widespread lack of understanding of design's uses and significance.

WEDGE

What has gone wrong? Society is no longer tightly defined by core values, for one thing, and modern culture is atomised, dispersed by factors as disparate as globalisation, mass media, immigration and consumerism. But perhaps the most obvious wedge between design and society is driven by detachment from the processes of making artifacts. Since the introduction of mass-production techniques, average people are no longer artisans or craftspeople. This removes them from an everyday engagement with design, which is simply the conceptualising and theorising process that underpins the making of something. Design is the thinking that precedes fabrication, whether of a garment or a space rocket. Modernism coincided with wholesale mass production, removing people from fabrication processes. And so design is remote from daily experience and understanding. It is seen as an arcane activity that can only be marginally appreciated, except by those inducted into its mysteries.

Our design approach emerges from an attitude or a process, not from any set of prescriptions

PRACTICALITY

Those who do appreciate the effects of good design realise that design matters: the well-balanced implement, the ergonomic chair, the life-enhancing house. Design is about practicality and making things work better. This is its primary role. In practice, though, design is commonly confused with style, which is an outcome of design, not its driver. Style is outward expression, providing cues that define an object in terms of the values of a particular era. Essentially style is about identity.

VISION

While fundamentally design is about making things better, more effective, 'smarter', it is also about presenting new possibilities and taking us where we have not been before. This is the visionary aspect of good design – not innovation for the sake of novelty, but the genuine creative leap of discovery that expands awareness and conceptual horizons.

QUALITY

Even if design's true nature as the ordering process governing effective fabrication (ingenuity, economical use of materials, and technical efficiency leading to the most comfortable/simple/satisfying outcome) is misunderstood, that does not prevent good designers from demonstrating the superior practical, commercial and psychological effects of design. Good design enriches experience.

DESIGN

This book is based on the premise that design matters and does have a vivid contribution to make to everyday life. The work of the Australian-based firm, Emery Vincent Design, demonstrates how design affects us at an everyday practical level in many different contexts – from the scale of a page to that of a whole city. In two decades, Emery Vincent Design has become a multidisciplinary, internationally acknowledged practice. Led by Garry Emery, it has produced a critical body of work hand-in-hand with a developed theoretical design approach. The practice represents that unusual entity – a design firm with equally sound commercial and cultural credentials. This book gathers together many of the writings of Emery Vincent Design expressing the central ideas and themes that shape the firm's design approach. There is no single defining style, but rather a way of working that leads to a certain signature. That way of working includes an eclectic design philosophy, a focus on new horizons, and a willingness to treat design as a collaborative project.

2

A design practice on the rim of the world

6   0

3

Emery Vincent Design

RIM

At first glance Australia might seem to be located on the fringe of things, tucked away in the southern Pacific. We don't, however, feel particularly isolated. We have a very vibrant urban existence and we are in touch with what's happening in the rest of the world. We travel, of course. And people come to visit us. So while a regional sensibility can perhaps be discerned, most design work in Australia is international in its scope and spirit.

INCOMPLETE

This idea of regional identity is vaguely current in design disciplines. It comes from two sources: from a contemporary ideological commitment to localism, and (in the case of postcolonial countries such as Australia) from a sense that the national psyche is still undeveloped or incomplete, which perhaps it is. (But we now live in an era when we understand that nothing is ever 'complete'.)

HETEROGENEOUS

We see the issue of an Australian identity in design as being bound up with some of the more notable physical qualities of this place – the openness, the brightness of the light, the hugeness of the distances. The other prime influence is the Australian capacity for eclecticism. Being a heterogeneous people (some 110 languages are spoken) and also being essentially pragmatic, we have no hesitation in appropriating and blending the most disparate ideas, flavours, references and attitudes. We are most definitely not purists.

ECLECTIC

Having said that, we are not sure that our work at Emery Vincent Design can be identified as being specifically 'Australian' beyond its being eclectic. In this it tends towards a graphic synthesis of different design cultures with references to European modernism and technology as well as the vibrant colours of a subtropical location. The essential elements in our design are typography, calligraphy and references to art, architecture and popular culture. We aim to work with a simple vocabulary to produce design solutions of relevance and strength, while searching for a way of establishing our own visual language, methods of communication and techniques, always more interested in the design process than style.

POLARITY

We prefer not to be connected to a particular school of design. If we have a philosophy, it's the sense that design ideas come from two opposing directions: from rationalism, or the legible organisation of information, and from surrealism, or the chance conjunction of unrelated images. Surrealism helps to communicate an idea with vitality and immediacy. Rationalism and surrealism are present throughout our work.

ESTABLISHED

Emery Vincent Design has been operating since 1980, when we established an office in Melbourne. We opened our Sydney office in 1987. Since then we have developed as a substantial and diversified design practice operating throughout Australia and also increasingly in Asia, with a stable team of forty-five people including graphic designers, architects, interior designers, a market researcher, a corporate identity strategist and multimedia designers. We work principally in three areas: corporate identity, brand identity and environmental graphic design. Our core business is graphic design.

COLLABORATION

Some designers consider collaboration between designers working in different disciplines to be a matter of compromise. But you cannot copyright an idea: ideas are available for everyone to develop. Whenever we work with other design specialists, we enjoy the opportunity to learn from their different disciplines and ideas. It's nearly always a positive experience, and we learn something with each new collaboration.

DISTANCE

Collaboration has a very important spin-off: it teaches you how to listen. When you listen well, you also develop critical detachment. You can distance yourself from an attachment to a particular approach or methodology and from a sense of ownership of an idea. We believe it's important as designers to cultivate this critical distance because it makes us free and helps us evaluate ideas. It also allows us to clarify and objectively assess our own work.

FLAT

Our character as a design practice is engendered by our management structure at Emery Vincent Design, which is as flat as we can make it. There is one principal in the Melbourne office and one in the Sydney office. Beyond that, everyone works on an equal footing, communicating directly with whomever he or she needs to. Everyone collaborates. This might seem relatively unremarkable, yet it's the cornerstone of our operating efficiency and our capacity to address difficult and disparate design challenges laterally. We keep the boundaries fluid.

APPROACH

There is no design orthodoxy that we subscribe to. We have a recognisable design approach, but it is not based on a rigid design methodology. It is more an expression of a core of design values that the practice instils through emphasising the need for historical and cultural research and design literacy, and through constantly, if obliquely, questioning the theoretical basis of what we are doing. Our design approach emerges from an attitude or a process, not from a set of prescriptions.

DEMOCRATIC

The way our studios are designed is important to the way we work. We have a democratic operation. There are no private offices. We all occupy the same large open-plan space. This openness and absence of hierarchy are central to how we work. There is no display of our work, nor any art on the walls. What we put on show is design as process, with the interaction of people being the essential focus.

CULTURE

We see our library as a main hub of the studio where we can relate what we are thinking about to the greater culture of design – researching historical precedents, understanding where references come from, how design develops, where the innovations are occurring. Ours is a visual culture in constant flux. We must understand our cultural past and also find relevant ways to express our own times. This is part of our cultural work as design professionals. Research isn't about nostalgia; it's often about story telling and reinterpreting the past in a contemporary context. In other words, by enabling us to know the past, research can help us develop new narratives and new visions.

SCOPE

The scale and scope of our work varies from postage stamps to large urban signage programs. About half is print-based and new media, and the other half is environmental graphics – design for the built environment. Typography is a fundamental element, and it's the thread running through our work.

NAVIGATION

Traditionally, the role of the designer was more concerned with form than content, whereas much of today's design is focused on navigating digital information. Wayfinding through printed pages is established through typographic hierarchies – words. However, on-screen design relies more on emblems and signs to guide readers through multiple levels and layers of information, often using meaningful graphic metaphors.

CHURN

Thoughtful design delivers certain concrete information, but it is often full of ideas and implications that extend beyond the concrete and obvious. The act of reading itself is now quite different from what it was before the television age. Today we operate in a world of over-information. The average attention span has shrunk to a matter of seconds. And communications are often simple visual codes and expressions. Serious information has to be conveyed in thirty-second television grabs. The division between information and entertainment is permanently blurred. The television age means pluralism and continual change. Images flicker and transform as we watch. They are momentary and gone, replaced by a constant supply of yet more changing images. We are dazed by the amount of overlaid information on offer. We cannot absorb it all. We simply catch fragments as they churn past.

GLOBAL

Our work cannot help expressing the spirit of the times – the zeitgeist – and it inevitably reflects the cultural global village we all inhabit thanks to television, international travel and instant communications. At the same time, at Emery Vincent Design we are conscious of responding to place and cultural nuance, with the possibility that something distinctive that is our own may evolve.

There are intangibles that don't show up on a balance sheet –
things like intelligence, judgment, a sense of humor, and energy level.
Those are the qualities I use to pick my own team

Jan Leshly, CEO, SmithKline Beecham, *Harvard Business Review*, September–October, 1995

Looking backwards towards the future

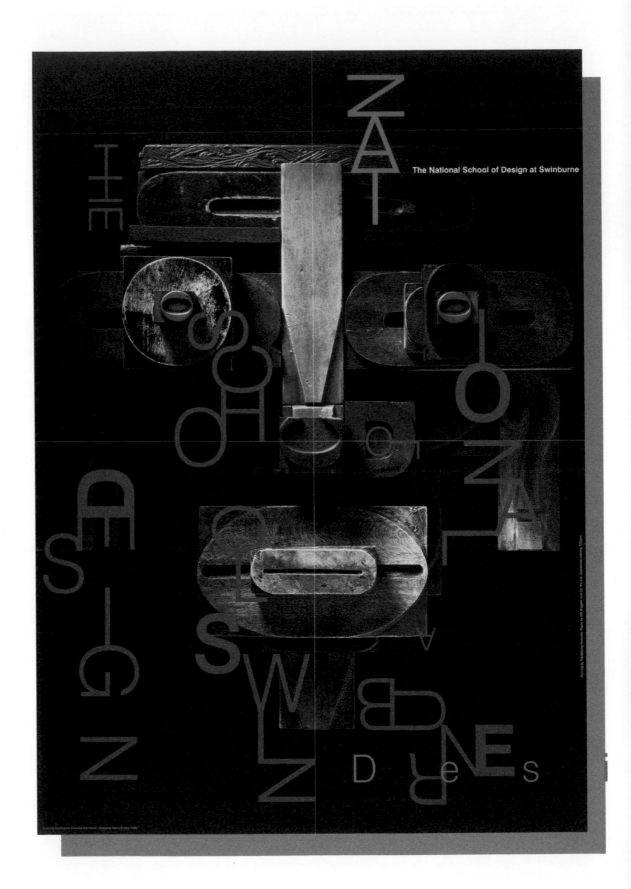

The National School of Design at Swinburne

Garry Emery

HARD CORE

A design philosophy is practical. It grows out of a way of working, out of the experience of doing, of failing and succeeding, of learning. Design cannot be reduced to formulae, and neither is there any single design philosophy. Each designer develops his or her own skills and ideas, and operates according to his or her own core feelings. It takes many years to develop this 'hard core'; this essential set of beliefs, feelings and attitudes that informs each design decision. Generally we are not conscious of it, but it operates at all times. This hard core is our philosophy.

My design philosophy comes out of a pragmatic apprenticeship in handcrafting letterforms. I believe that the highly developed coordination between hand and eye is essential among a good designer's skills. I also believe that an extensive understanding of the history of design is necessary for every good designer. And I believe that a good designer never stops learning new skills and new techniques and developing new ideas. Essentially, this is a philosophy of eclecticism: of being open to all ideas yet prepared to accept none except on the basis of my own experimentation and adaptation.

The essence of a designer's hard core is a real desire to communicate: to explain, to teach, and most importantly, to reveal. This matter of revelation is about exposing ideas through design so that the readers/viewers themselves 'invent' or develop the meaning of the work. In the process, they themselves become designers for that moment. It's about engaging the reader and generating interpretations.

A philosophy is a belief system. But you still have to put your beliefs into action, which is what every designer tries to do. This requires the development of tactics and methodological rules: a heuristic. In my case these heuristics are based on surrealism, modernism, abstraction, minimalism, the calligraphic gesture, and technology.

We must understand our cultural past and also find relevant ways to express our own times

Prof Haig Beck and Jackie Cooper

DAUNTING

Eighty Market Street, Southbank, appears on the outside as a typical industrial building; its rendered unpainted facade is raw and grey. Yet this isn't just another shed or warehouse. It is ornamented by a purposeful, oddly delicate grid of tiny galvanised steel tiles – a reticent indication of an intellectual overlay, which suggests that: Here is a place of design. The facade is a subtly decorated billboard. Inside the entry lobby, the staircase to the studio above is a big surprise. It is ostensibly a monumental staircase. But the materials are hardly grand: raw concrete and rough sheet steel, owing more to Escher than to Michelangelo. There are three flights. The central flight terminates in a trompe-l'oeil dead-end, and the authentic looking flight off to the right also proves to be barren. Obviously it's the left flight that leads to the studio, but this certainty is undermined by the provisional steel 'fiddlesticks' that constitute the handrails, not to mention the daunting hollow clanging of footsteps as even the most carefully placed shoes resonate on the bare metal treads.

This is like no staircase you've climbed before: ambiguous and disruptive, it redefines the experience of climbing a stair. The tolerable discomfort of the singular and loudly resonating metal stair sensitises the visitor to his or her self, diminishing the cool outer business persona that strives for constant control and poise. Your cool is frustrated by the knowledge that everyone above can hear your progress; already you are the object of curiosity long before you have the advantage of sighting your goal.

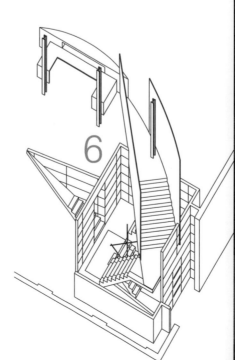

6

A walk on the wild side

1

The intention is to disengage visitors from previous preconceptions, to prepare them for a new experience in which their commercial expectations are balanced against the aesthetic and cultural imperatives of the design studio.

On reaching the top of these dramatic stairs, the entire office is gained in a sweeping glance. The architecture makes it clear how the studio workshop is organised and how things work. The studio layout is structured by a wide 'street' with 'buildings' down one side and the designers working in their 'front gardens' opposite. At the far end of the street is a 'park', a large open courtyard. Glancing around, it is apparent from the open plan (with everyone visible and the democratic design team hierarchy obvious) that what is on show here is process, how design is done, work in progress. Emery Vincent Design presents graphic design not as a finished product but as a cultural and professional process.

The 'buildings' lining the 'street' house the cultural, conference and service functions of the studio. Most prominent is the library. Unlike the white-clad buildings, the library is faced with galvanised metal panels in a rusticated pattern. The library is the focal hub of the working area: an accessible, functioning embodiment of the notion that graphic design depends on an awareness of the history and culture of typography and design.

Everyone collaborates
Openness and absence
of hierarchy are central to
how we work

Denton Corker Marshall Architects

3

A question of identity

Dr Peter Steidl

PERCEPTION

Identity is a major factor in all work undertaken by Emery Vincent Design. Who we are designing for? What perceptions are being generated? Perceptions influence attitudes, opinions and behaviour. Perceptions are the most powerful factor in decision making, so it is not surprising that the management of perceptions is a major issue for individuals and organisations alike. Perceptions have always been important. But people (at least in Western countries) now have much higher degrees of freedom to be who they want to be – or to appear to be who they want others to think they are – than ever before. They are free to create their own identities.

DESTINY

Historically, people were born into religions, trades, castes and other communities from which they couldn't generally escape. Being part of a community largely defined a person's identity. Symbols or visual identities expressed the attributes and values of these communities. These symbols were often literal and tangible, such as tools, weapons, castles and so on.

INCLINATION

In our post-industrialised world, people generally are not born into fixed communities that determine their identity. They are born into situations that can limit the range of possibilities open to them, but by and large leave them free to create their own identity within a given set of opportunities. With the change from what was almost deterministic in terms of people's identity to what is a fairly open system, there is naturally also a change in the importance of symbols people use to define themselves. People either want to express the way they are, ie express their actual identity, or they want to manipulate the way they are perceived. ie create a perception that they have certain qualities and attributes which they in fact do not have. Either way, they have to use symbolism to express their identity.

MEMBERSHIP

In defining a contemporary person's identity, it is, of course, possible to use the same sorts of symbols that served people in the past: symbols expressing membership of a church, citizenship of a country or a city, or of a trade or profession. But how effective are these symbols in a society where belonging to a church or being a tailor no longer defines identity absolutely? Obviously there are some exceptions, symbols that are still meaningful, such as the title 'Doctor' on a business card, the crucifix on a necklace, or the country club sticker on the windscreen. However, we generally cannot learn much that is relevant to the way we judge people by simply knowing more about the communities to which they belong. This is because, firstly, membership of the traditional communities we are born into has become for many a passive membership: we may still nominally belong to a church, but we are not active in it; we do live in a city, but this has little impact on our lives. Secondly, we can readily leave a community – we can adopt another religion, live in another city or country, change our trade or profession. Our identity is mutable.

DEFINING

What has largely replaced the symbols we use to express our identity or to create desired image perceptions can now be found in other spheres of life. In tune with the commercialisation of society and the underlying free market thinking, we increasingly regard symbols related to consumption as important. Where we buy our clothes, which fashion designers we favour, which restaurants we are seen in, which films we have seen, which car we drive, or where we spend our holidays tells us more about a person in this commercial society than their often 'inherited' religion or their parent's trade or profession. Inextricably linked to a society that has learned to take cues about people's identity from their consumption habits are the symbols that express the qualities of the products, services and organisations that are the objects of such consumption. The brands we buy, the company we work with or invest in reflect, or at least seem to reflect, our own identities.

BRANDS

People present themselves like products in well-designed packages. Brands symbolise particular styles, qualities, attributes and values. This applies to corporations as much as to product brands. By associating ourselves with these brands, we are able to express our own identity – or pretend to have certain qualities even if we don't have them. Clearly not all consumption is determined by a desire to express your identity or to generate a particular image. Nor are all jobs taken or investments made on the basis of which company I want to associate myself with. Yet we will be judged by many on the basis of these relationships, and those who want to create a particular image will often use these relationships to make their point. And let's not forget that the market research industry attempts to segment us all using our relationships with brands and corporations as important factors in identifying these new types of 'community'.

PROVENANCE

Over and above the definition of personal and commercial identities are other significant forms of identity that impinge on design. The overarching matter of a national identity, on the one hand, and the more locally focused issue of sense of place, on the other, are two extremes of an identity continuum that operates constantly on design. Fundamentally, all design is about identity. Design sets out to communicate effectively; and meaningful communication depends on a compact between a sender and a receiver in which the identity of the sender is at least vaguely acknowledged. Without this kernel of identification, a message – like an orphan – is without provenance. How may we evaluate it?

CONTEXT

Identity is the hinge about which messages are communicated and design decisions revolve. In designing signage for a new city, or in deploying design as an active agent in the definition of sense of place in a cultural institution, for instance, it is identity that establishes the basis for design decisions. This can mean one of two things: that the ensuing design endeavours to augment and enhance sense of place, or that it deliberately imposes a seamless international context that eradicates the existing local context. The latter occurs the world over wherever such commercial behemoths as McDonald's or Coca-Cola put down roots, precisely in order to accentuate perception of their global power by obliterating the pre-existing surroundings. Or the obliteration of local context occurs wherever it is deemed that excitement/dynamism/attraction is likely to be generated by an exotic – ie, non-local – context. This is the reason shopping malls generally define themselves in terms of a glitzy 'international' identity (although there is also a contrary marketing trend towards creating a more 'local' sense of place by recreating the experience of shopping in a village).

Context is a prevailing and significant factor to be reckoned with in all design. Architects are well aware of this. Context includes a variety of elusive factors such as local climate, quality of light, orientation, flora and fauna, cuisine, culture, social patterns and so on. It's to do with what makes a place a place, different from other places. The theme of alienation generated by featureless suburban sprawls in part owes something to the eradication of place and replacement of it with a sanitised, formula-driven built environment – one largely devoid of any local or specific identity.

Context also provides a baseline for graphic design. In evaluating a brief, the designer pays heed to the circumstances and physical context within which the brief has been formulated and the design must operate. In the case of environmental graphics, context is literally the background against which a design occurs: contextual cues are identified either to confirm or deny context, or otherwise comment on it. But context is always a strong element to contend with.

Design is the link
between commerce and innovation

Issey Miyake in Mark Holborn, *Issey Miyake*, Benedikt Taschen Verlag, 1995, p16

EMERY VINCENT DESIGN

1996

red hot

1996 Award of Excellence, New York Type Directors Club
1997 Award of Honour, Design Zentrum, Essen

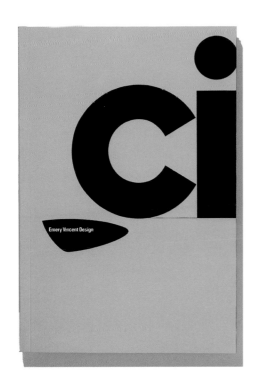

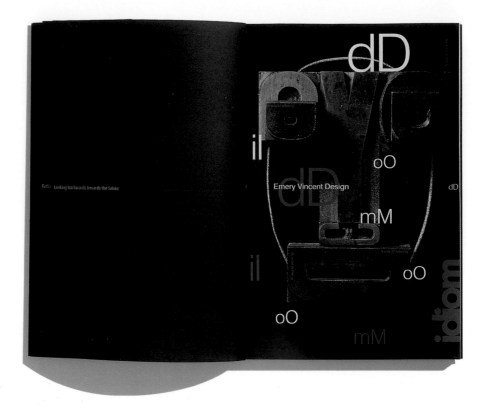

1999 Certificate of Typographic Excellence, New York Type Directors Club

A landmark for the city of Melbourne and a landmark project
for Emery Vincent Design. The presentation of all communications
for the Centre had to be legible, comprehensive and accessible
to the broadest range of people, including local and international
exhibitors and visitors

MELBOURNE EXHIBITION CENTRE

1006

The architecture
and the graphics are
unified. In a way,
the primary signage
is so well integrated
with the architecture
that it is difficult to
discern whether they
are sign panels or
architectural elements

Homage to constructivism

It's all very large-scale and robust, which has to do
with the building's program and the fact that thousands
of people are moving through at any given moment.
The graphics themselves are highly decorative,
very colourful and strong. There probably aren't too
many buildings where there is an opportunity for the
graphics to be expressed in this forthright manner

The architects, Denton Corker Marshall, designed the
long frontage facing the river as a civic verandah,
reinterpreting the old classical architectural idea of the
colonnade. The bold blade forms that punctuate the
glazed walls at odd angles signify entry points, and to
these were applied super-sized graphics to match
the architectural scale

A major civic building contributes to the city's
identity and sense of place

The stencilled typeface has been custom-designed
for the identity. It alludes to the maritime history
of the site and also the constructive raw nature of
the architecture

1997 Award of Honour, Design Zentrum, Essen

QUEENSLAND NEWSPAPERS PAVILION EXPO 88

1988

Visual identity, signage
program, exhibition graphics
and merchandising

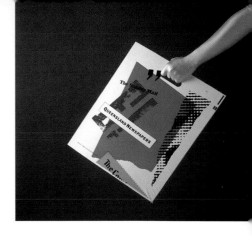

Exhibition design reminiscent of the work of early modernists
such as Piet Zwart and El Lissitzky

The graphic imagery refers to newspaper banners and headline typefaces, continuous
sheet printing, half-tone imagery and serrated newsprint edges

Providing sense of place where there is none by illustrating the main attractions at the Stadium: football and track and field events

Sixty-five metres of
super-sized graphic imagery
for the 1958 Olympic stadium
refurbished by
Peter Elliott Architects

A three-dimensional
graphic wall to screen
a banal stadium

OLYMPIC PARK STADIUM, MELBOURNE

1998

Environmental or architectural graphic design is a highly
specialised field. Success depends on the close productive
collaboration of graphic designer and architect or interior designer.
Effective architectural graphic design enhances the external
and internal architecture it serves, announcing its presence and
ambience, and clearly informing and directing the public

Super-sized letterforms

The sign was designed in collaboration with
Ashton Raggatt McDougall Architects. Collaboration
can be exciting: searching for immediate
solutions, taking risks and being prepared to fail,
and recognising and exploiting the accidental

A contextually disruptive insertion
into a suburban street

1996 Annual Award, Tokyo Typo Directors Club

ASHTON RAGGATT McDOUGALL ARCHITECTS

1989

OCT 17 –
NOV 2
96

Melbourne
Festival

The textural surface
of the sheet metal
is achieved by hand
routing, following
a photocopy template
of a technical botanical
drawing of a leaf

To advertise the location of a bar and restaurant.
A stylised letter b and leaf form – a reference to the
adjacent Royal Melbourne Botanic Gardens

BOTANICAL HOTEL, MELBOURNE

1987

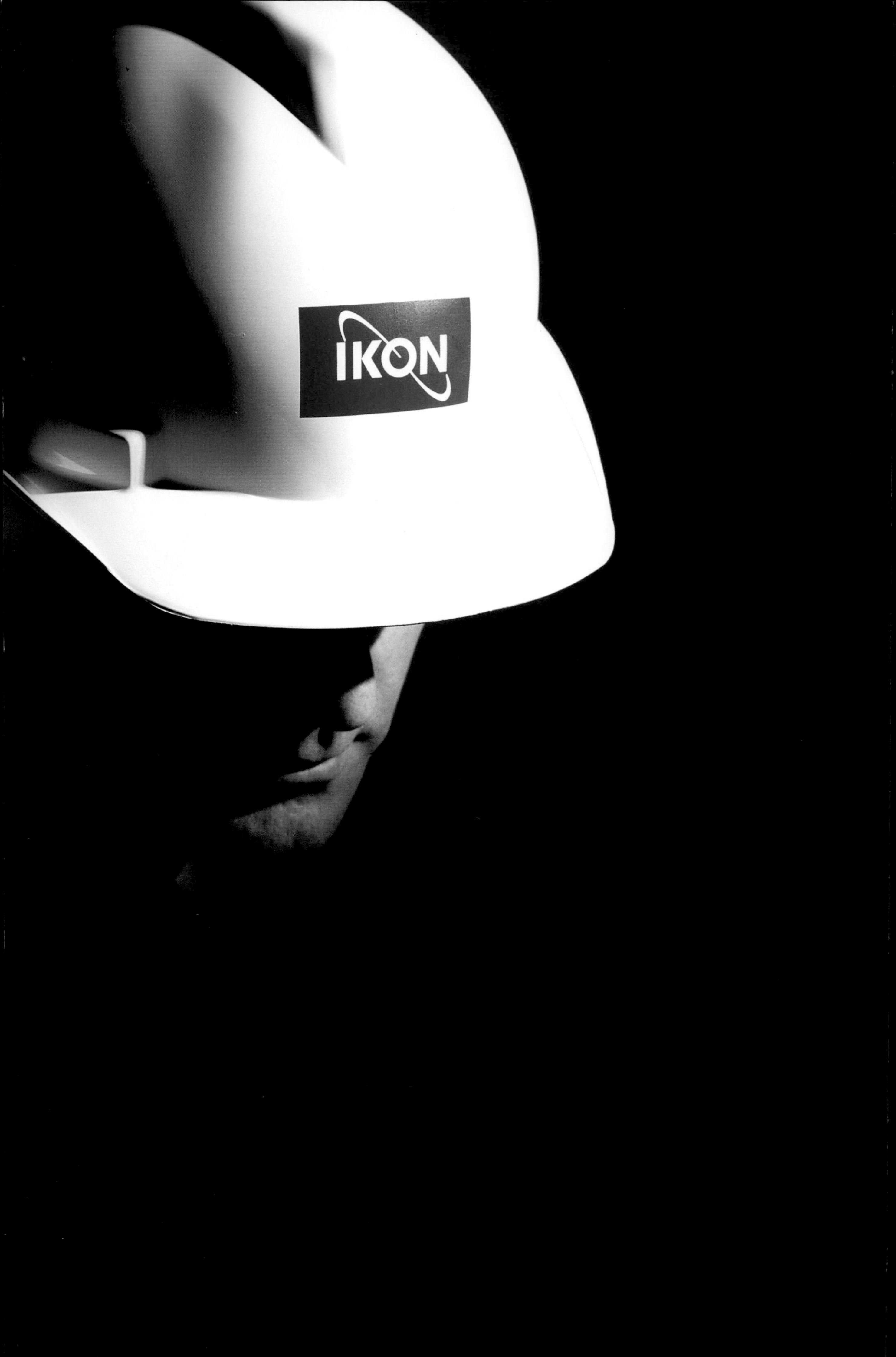
IKON

1997
1989

A S T A

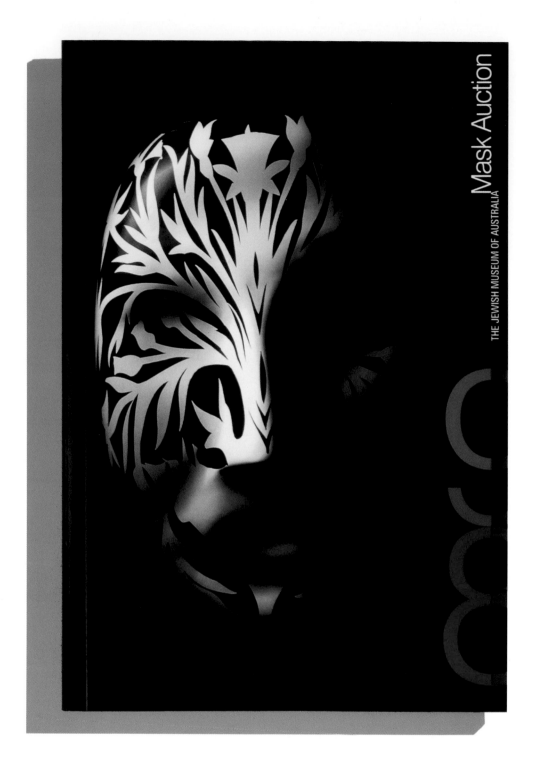

Mask Auction

THE JEWISH MUSEUM OF AUSTRALIA

1999 Gold Medal Award, *Creativity 28*, USA

A catalogue of masks decorated by artists
for a fund-raising auction

JEWISH MUSEUM OF AUSTRALIA

1998

WORKSHOP 3000

1989 to 1999

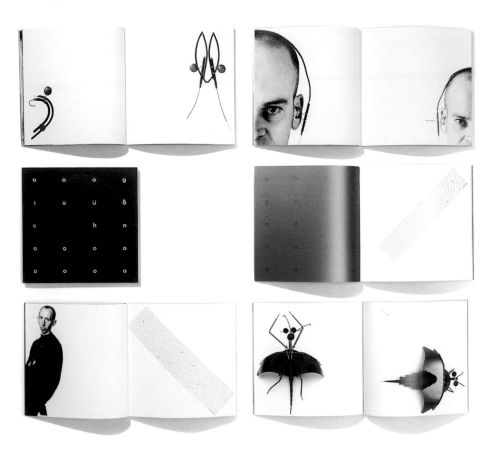

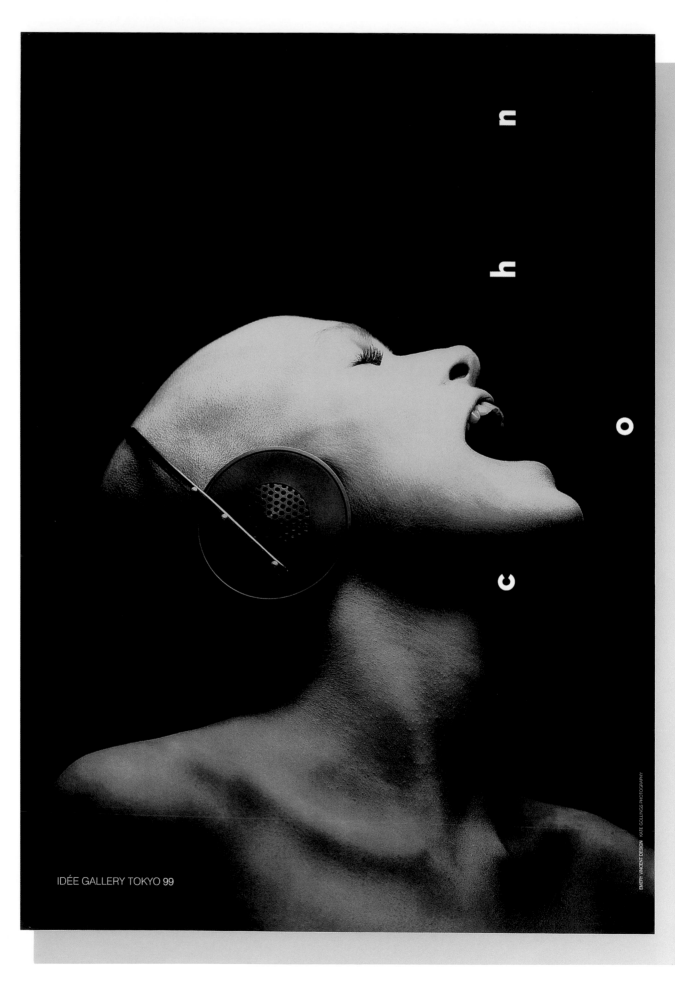

n

h

o

c

IDÉE GALLERY TOKYO 99

Just because you send a particular
message doesn't mean that it will be received
in the way you intended

o   o   o   o

o   o   o   o

c   h   n

o   o   o   o

o   o   o   o

Production work: Earrings. Another of Cohn's hallmarks is the flat disc earrings. These resulted from the designer's intention to make production line jewellery that was immediately viable. Also, with the image of 'mass' production firmly enmeshed in Cohn's aesthetic brows though her work in mostly highly crafted lines are work appeals to a wide. The discs are manufactured on an extraordinary range of anodised colours available for one central fitting. The colours have been devised by Cohn in the course of her constant routing of pressed and torsion discs

Catalogue for Susan Cohn exhibition in Japan

Modernist in spirit, clear, dynamic
and disruptive: the graphic design
speaks of the jewellery

The jewellery pieces are reproduced at actual size without shadows, and float
on the page in abstracted space, increasing the effect of spareness and contemplation.
The catalogue is black and white, apart from four bold coloured images.
The unconventional page numbering consists of progressively lengthening lines
of dots down the side of each page

The inclusion of two languages is
treated as a virtue: they are
counterposed as compositional blocks
held in dynamic tension on the page,
each highlighting the other's otherness,
neither taking precedence

1992 Gold Award, Tokyo Typo Directors Club,
Judges' comments: 'fresh, crisp balance
in page composition of photographs and text'

Toscano Architects
Corporate and brand identity
for a Japanese food manufacturer

Stylised sun symbol with Japanese characteristics

SAKATA

1995

Smart companies have always realised
that their identity matters as much
as their actual products or services,
and they have to get across that identity
in a marketplace that is teeming with
other commercial entities competing for
attention and recognition – and profits

AUSTRALIAN NATIONAL MARITIME MUSEUM, SYDNEY

1991

The name of the museum
is communicated in semaphore.
Detail of the metal panels
which pivot in the wind

Everything signifies

A hybrid: sign and kinetic installation

Designing for three dimensions is different from designing
in two dimensions. Many principles are the same: balance, order,
composition. But the techniques are often quite different.
In three-dimensional graphic design, which includes identification
signage and wayfinding information, it is not appropriate to simply
scale up a two-dimensional concept. A three-dimensional,
spatial premise is required

SOUTHGATE, MELBOURNE

1990

Urban space Architectural scale Legibility Landmark   Place making

Menara

Menara 1 PETRONAS
Menara 2 PETRONAS
Dewan Filharmonik PETRONAS
Taman KLCC

Menara Maxis
Mandarin Oriental Hotel
Suria KLCC
PETROSAINS
Galeri PETRONAS

Tempat Letak Kereta KLCC
Bas dan Teksi

Architects Cesar Pelli and Associates
Landscape architects Roberto Burle Marx

Design of the wayfinding and signage program for
a landmark central city redevelopment comprising the
Petronas Twin Towers, a retail complex, concert hall,
16.2 hectare urban park, and mosque

KUALA LUMPUR CITY CENTRE

1996

The sign signals its presence through inflated scale and constitutes a sculptural landmark on the street

KLCC Humanist: A typeface for urban signage custom-designed to express cultural nuances

Modernism
Arabic calligraphic gestures
Islamic geometric principles
Harmony

Vessel

A square base extruded, narrowed, twisted,
tilted and sliced at an angle

EMERY VINCENT DESIGN

1997

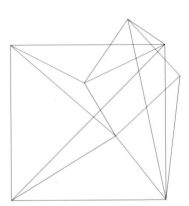

Denton Corker Marshall Architects

Lightweight portable sign stabilised by two removable aluminium rods

AUSTRALIAN EMBASSY, TOKYO

1990

AUSTRALIAN EMBASSY, BEIJING

1991

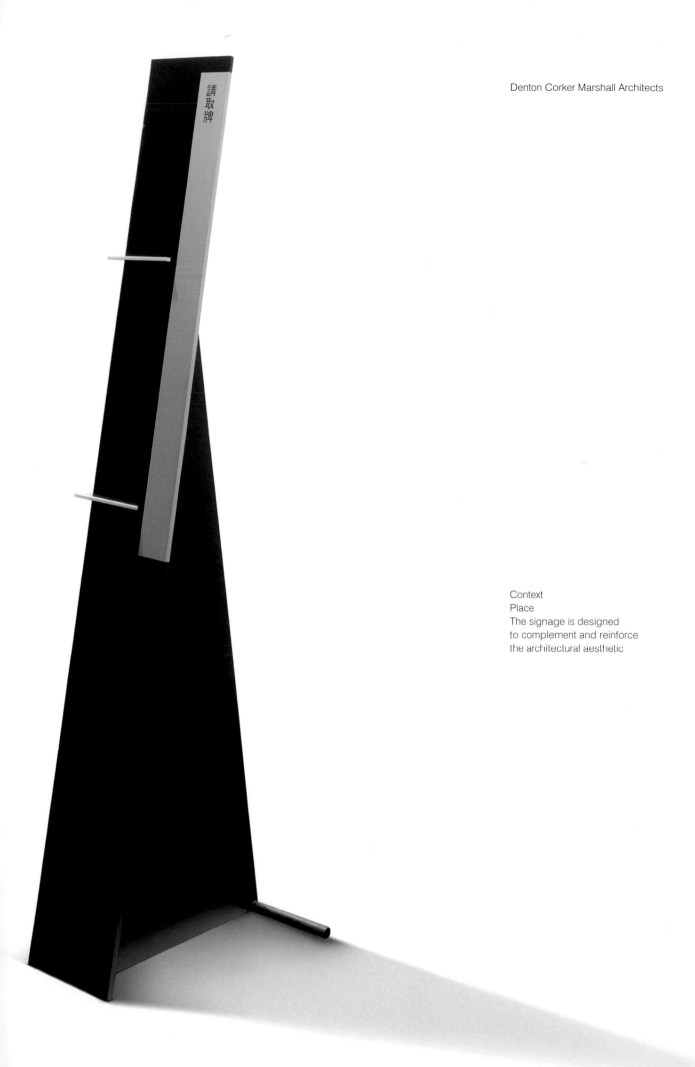

請取牌

Denton Corker Marshall Architects

Context
Place
The signage is designed
to complement and reinforce
the architectural aesthetic

We work side by
side with companies
to help them to
conceive, implement
and manage strategic
changes to their
businesses and
identities, or to market
or launch products
and services

Rejuvenation

AUSTRALIA POST

1999

A corporate image is revamped and rationalised, but the well-known
symbol is not lost. The P logo, the pillar box red and the word POST are
reinforced and clarified into a memorable combination

Hassell Architects
Building identification Wayfinding Signage

The terrazzo base of the freestanding
metal sign matches the flooring material
and reflects the architectural aesthetic,
integrating signage and building

COMMONWEALTH LAW COURTS, MELBOURNE

1998

1999

Letterforms spray-painted onto expanded metal panel: the letters appear and disappear according to the light and people's movement past the building

ART & DESIGN

The gridded plane is exploited as a billboard for building identification: signage and architecture are integrated

Minimalist

Faculty of Art a

POWERHOUSE MUSEUM, SYDNEY

1988

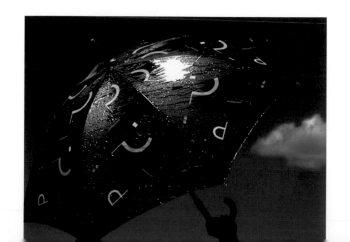

New South Wales
Government Architects Branch

Visual identity
From the architectural scale of the building down   Signage and wayfinding
to the exhibition labelling, a coherent image   Merchandising
Marketing communications
Exhibition labelling

Constructivist
Abstraction
Deconstructing
the parts

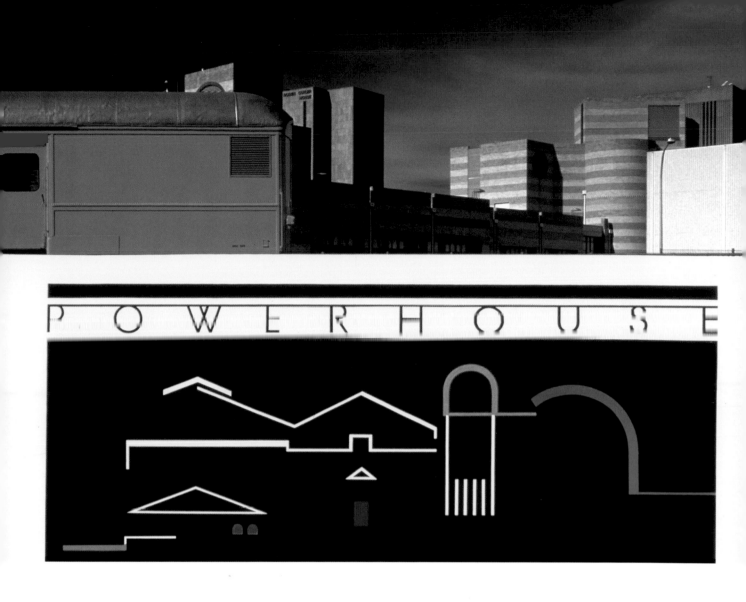

The Powerhouse museum is a collection of old industrial
buildings knitted together with a new architectural intervention.
We used the buildings' profiles to generate a memorable identity
which can be used whole or as fragmented parts

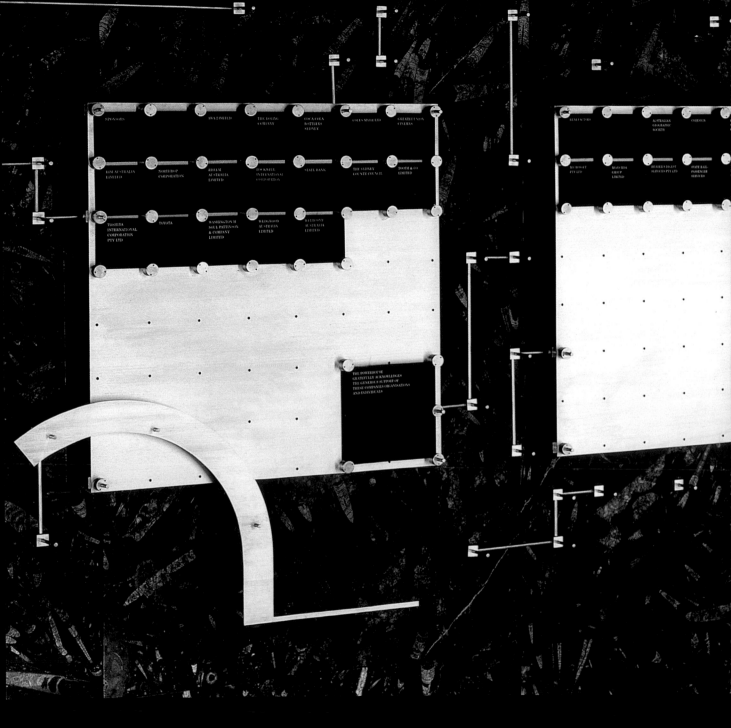

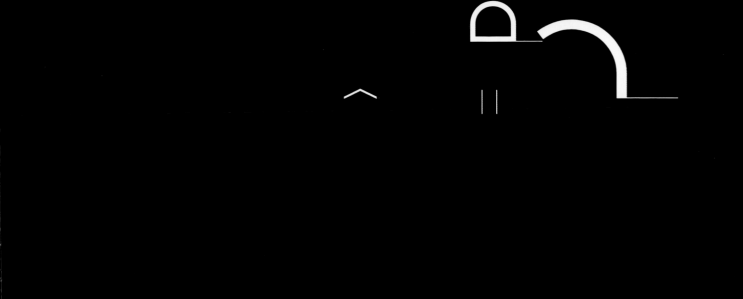
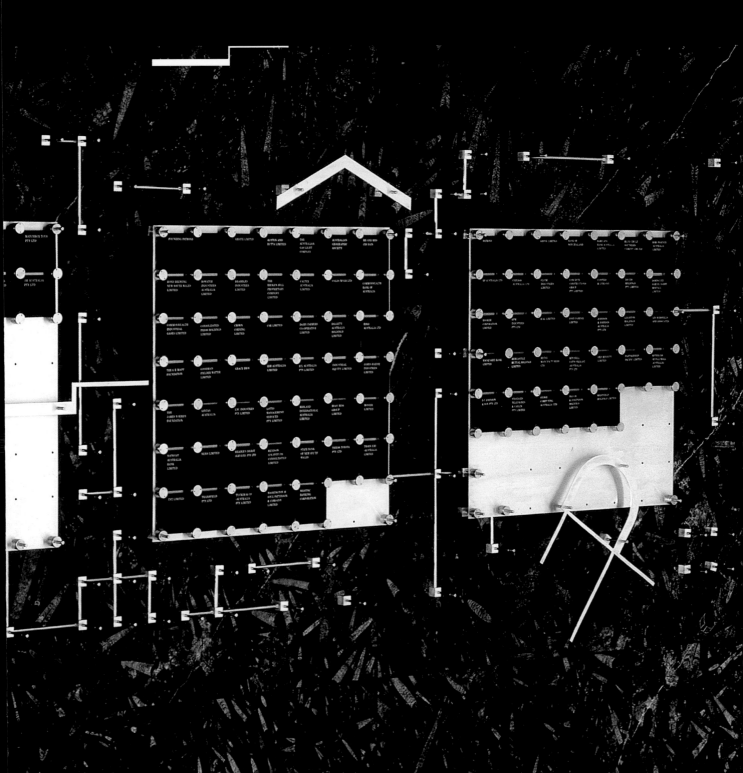

HASSELL GROUP

1993

THE UNIVERSITY OF MELBOURNE

It's not what you see that is art; it is the gap. — Marcel Duchamp

potter

THE IAN POTTER MUSEUM OF ART, MELBOURNE

1998

The graphics transcend the task of sign: they mesh the functions of sign, screen and identity, and form an enigmatic layering to the glazing. The text – statements from artists – is treated as decoration. It compositionally operates in both horizontal and vertical directions. From the exterior, the graphics locate the gallery's cafe and provide it with an identity

3 Administration

2 Gallery and study room

1 Gallery

G Gallery, cafe and toilets

Katsalidis Architects
Logo, building graphics and signage, special
graphics for gallery spaces and a new cafe, marketing
materials, promotional publications and catalogues

Constructivist graphics El Lissitzky
Dutch modernism Piet Zwart and De Stijl

As designers we understand architecture's role in
signalling identity and cultural intentions, and also the functional
issues associated with buildings such as lighting, approach
and entry, circulation, sight lines, the psychology of colour,
traffic engineering and landscaping

At the Museum's entrance,
a LED scrolling sign displays digital
information about events and
exhibitions. This use of a commercial
signage element for a cultural
institution is a disruptive tactic that
heightens perception of the Museum
as lively and contemporary

Partnership

potter

Transport and parking
Trams deliver you right at the door of The Potter on Swanston Street
Visitors with disabilities should ring The Potter the day before to arrange parking
After 5pm parking is available on The University grounds (gate 1) for a $2 coin
Admission
Admission to The Potter is free
Admission charges apply for special exhibitions and events
(members admitted free)

Swanston Street Parkville
Victoria 3052 Australia
Telephone 613 9344 5148
Facsimile 613 9344 4484
s.epskamp@art-museum.unimelb.edu.au
www.art-museum.unimelb.edu.au

THE UNIVERSITY OF MELBOURNE

The Ian Potter Museum of Art

" The Potter is defining the meaning of art in our
society and giving significance to Australian culture
in the global community "

opening hours

Tuesday to Wednesday 10am to 5pm
Thursday 12pm to 9pm
Friday to Sunday 10am to 5pm
Closed Mondays

THE UNIVERSITY OF
MELBOURNE
Australia

The signage and graphics respond to the architectural themes of
the building in terms of formal composition, colours and design ethos.
The architectural play of stainless steel and rusting corten is picked
up in the silver and orange of the graphics. The logo makes direct
reference to the distinctive cut-away corner of the building's main facade:
it is an abstracted two-dimensional representation of the architecture

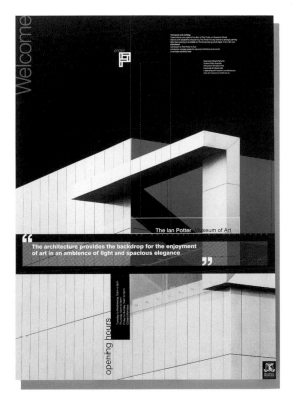

Degrees of cool
Reticence and the appeal of cold beauty

REFLECTIONS ON MINIMALISM

1997 Award for Excellence, Tokyo Typo Directors Club

Gallery Funaki 1996

Reticence in design – isn't that the whole essence of what design is about? I mean, we talk about elegance as being perhaps the highest mark that a designer might aim for. Elegance is a lot more than just a way of talking about style, a way of saying that something is cool. The word actually has a mathematical precision. It means, simply, to achieve the maximum effect with the minimum of effort. This idea of reticence or cool very much includes elegance, or minimalism if you like, because design is ultimately about achieving the maximum by using the minimum. If you are looking for the reason why reticence in design has a compelling appeal, there it is. Less is more, as we know from Mies. Minimalism expresses the essence of things, which always has the power to be deeply satisfying. But minimalism isn't something that derives from heroic modernism. It has always been around, in all cultures and epochs, depending on the prevailing cultural milieu for its particular expression. Even if we know nothing about a culture or an era, we can still instantly recognise and understand its good design through minimalism. The central role of minimalism in design has never varied. Great artists and designers have always expressed powerful ideas with the greatest economy. They make the essence of something apparent through a gesture, an attitude, a simple, clarifying statement. We can think equally of the sinuous simplicity of the cats of Pharoanic statuary or Caravaggio's depictions of excess and debauch as being elegant statements of their respective times and cultures. The point is that minimalism takes many forms, depending on its particular cultural circumstances. What we typically understand as minimalism today is the product of our modern age of abstraction, which itself pares things right down. So we have minimalism in an age of abstraction representing a meta-minimal design ethos.

The currency of minimalism is simplicity. Simplicity can be perceived as alienating because it is so strong and confronting – whereas complexity and embellishment offer refuge in the familiar and comfortable and connect us with feelings of nostalgia. For that reason, minimalism is rejected by the majority. Ando's architecture represents the epitome of the strength of simplicity. He manipulates space, light and form, creating stark spaces that offer a rare opportunity to experience light in its purest form, without the interference of objects. Ando shows us that space is not emptiness: it is full, the opposite of nothingness. The presence of absence. In the same way, silence is not nothingness. It depends on sound to exist. The idea of opposites, polarities, interacting to create an integrated whole is fundamental to all human creativity and meaning. So form depends on space for definition: the object does not exist without space, and vice versa. Similarly, two-dimensional space is made dynamic by the tension between the mark and the field, and the placement of each against the other, negative and positive. Virtual space is enriched by the illusion of nearness and distance. Reticence, emptiness, even nihilism: these are design values that we implicitly understand in these modern, abstract times. Emptiness and stillness are valued also by various mystic traditions, from Western monastic orders to Zen Buddhism. Design, with its mundane functional and representational imperatives, finds a profound philosophical counterpart in the spiritual contemplative realm, beyond emotion and beyond style. What we might describe as melancholic, dislocated or stripped of warmth and familiarity – in other words, some of the more extreme versions of contemporary minimalism – are examples of design that are steeped in the deeper perennial imperative to plumb what is essential. This is at the core of all good design – and why we as designers need to value and understand the deeper purpose of elegance. **Garry Emery, published in *Funnel* '97**

2

← South wing
→ North wing

Design concept

Architects
Mario Bellini Associati and Metier 3

NATIONAL GALLERY OF VICTORIA, MELBOURNE

1999

Denton Corker Marshall Architects

Primary identification for the museum entry
Horizontal tonal variances in the glass panels
Monumental scale

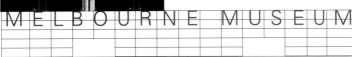

MELBOURNE MUSEUM

The architecture is rational, elegant and devoid of decoration beyond the fastidious detailing of materials, textures and colours. The architectural language is about planes and the joining of elements Every part has a rational purpose, and the seams of the building become its decoration. In the context of such carefully detailed architecture, the signage is designed to constitute another layer in this system of jointed elements

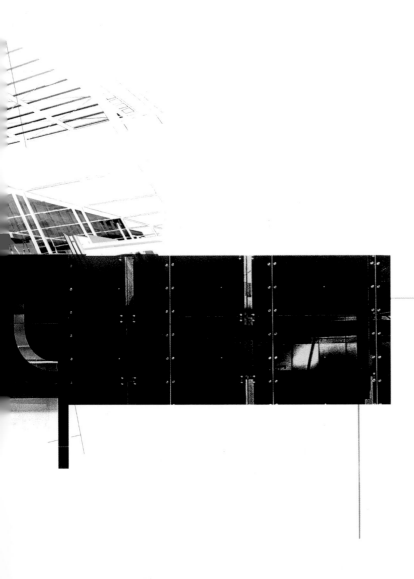

Architects Lawrence Nield & Partners
Landscape architects Spackman & Mossop

Calligraphic references

Palimpsest
Acid-etched metal with enamel-filled colour
Contemporary interpretation of historic imagery
relevant to this site at the heart of Sydney's
colonial past

COOK + PHILLIP PARK, SYDNEY

1999

Urban place making Materiality Memory

A primary identifier for an urban
park incorporating pools, gymnasium
and recreation centre

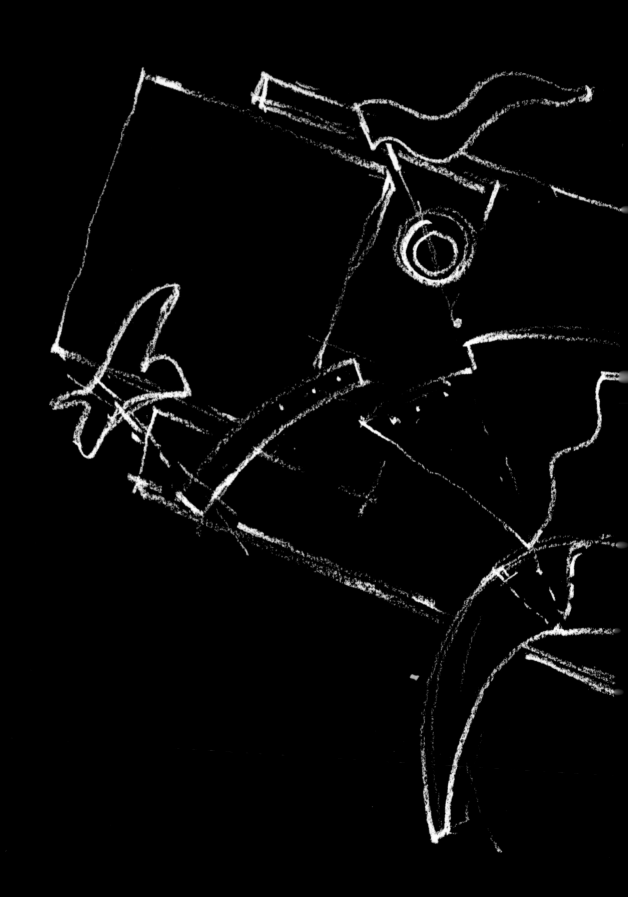

ROYAL ALEXANDRA HOSPITAL FOR CHILDREN, SYDNEY

1995

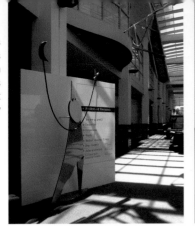

Architects
Lawrence Nield & Partners
McConnel Smith & Johnson
epartment of Public Works and Services
Woods Bagot
Ancher Mortlock & Woolley

The graphics help to modulate the vast and alienating scale of the hospital and provide a welcoming element for sick children and anxious parents

The familiar utilitarian hospital signage of the 1960s, using Helvetica type, has given way to expectations of patients, workers and visitors for more memorable and amusing imagery to mitigate the sombre institutional connotations of a hospital

Circulation routes are treated as 'streets' with street names and little 'squares' or 'parks' (landscaped courtyards) opening off them, with recognisable 'landmarks' that help people orient themselves and remember where to go. The landmarks are structural, sculptural forms incorporating directions

Graphics are an aid to communication and not simply an illustrative prop

1996 Merit Award, Society for Environmental Graphic Design, USA
1997 Award of Honour, Design Zentrum, Essen

Otto is a simple stainless steel table. Designed as a work table for the Emery Vincent Design studio, it is easily carried by one person. One leg is adjustable to ensure stability on any surface

We make no claim to be industrial designers. However we enjoy experimenting with three-dimensional form: it's an aspect of our research. Otto serves a practical function in our studio. We have also designed an exhibition display system, Plato's Cube, as well as a vessel. Designing these objects stretches us as designers and keeps us limber

Using materials which are durable, recyclable and easy to manufacture

EMERY VINCENT DESIGN

1998

The table is equally appropriate for commercial, industrial and domestic environments. It lives just as happily outdoors as indoors

Otto is basic and minimal

Woods Bagot Architects

This corporate display is created by subjecting numerous disparate archival images from the company's records to a process of visual degradation, bringing them all into a common graphic language of deconstruction. The fragmented images form a multilayered palimpsest nearly seven metres high. The aluminium panels are acid-etched and paint-filled and polished to a patina. The images, no longer literal, are decorative and ambiguous

FOSTERS BREWING GROUP, MELBOURNE

1994 to 1998

Scale and repetition
A grand crescendo is created by the
repetition of simple elements

1998 Design Distinction Award, Annual Design Review, *ID* magazine, New York
Judges' comments:
'I can't figure out how to categorize this.'
'Its minimal use of materials creates an incredible effect. It's spatial,
advertising-oriented and informational.'
'You see a lot of corporate graphics, you see a lot of messaging
in the graphics, but this is one of the very few we've seen that creates
an environment and gives off a radiance.'
'It's so strong considering so little was used.'

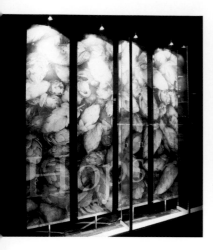 

A story of the land and
the raw materials of brewing.
The display panels are
seen from the street as well as
from the interior spaces

In the corporate headquarters
there is a delicate interaction between
graphic design, the architecture and
the interior design, each contributing
to the overall impact

1997 Good Design Award, Chicago Athanaeum,
Museum of Architecture and Design, Chicago

A design solution that answers the need for information, spatial definition
and decoration, and the vital projection of a corporate image

PACIFIC POWER

1992

The bundle of qualities expressed
through a symbol or logo
embodies an organisation's core values
and differentiating characteristics.
The corporate identity projects
a qualitative statement that customers,
employees and other key target groups
identify with and associate
with the organisation

POWER

CARMEN FURNITURE

1990 to 1995

The office furniture system for the 21st century
Showrooms in Sydney, Melbourne, Canberra, Brisbane, Adelaide, Hobart, Darwin, Perth

Carmen VOKO

V10

design excellence

versatility,

user comfort,

Rational layout,

Carmen

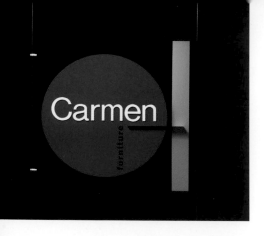

Visual identity
Marketing communications
Product brochures
Advertising

Constructivism
Surrealism
Homage to Matisse and Magritte

If I have a philosophy, it's the sense that design ideas
come from two opposing directions: from rationalism – or the
legible organisation of information; and from surrealism
– or the chance conjunction of images. Surrealism helps to
communicate an idea with vitality and immediacy. Rationalism
and surrealism are present throughout our work

Garry Emery

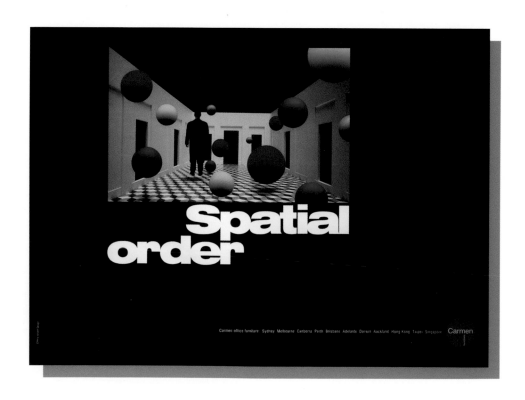

Office seating systems

CarmenVERVE

Carmen

1994 Gold Award, Biennale of Graphic Design, Brno

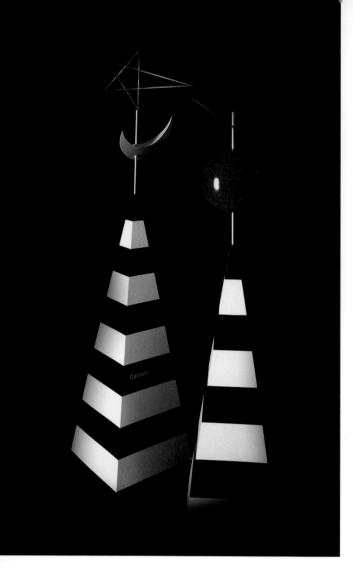

Disruption

In our work there is a strong leaning towards the lateral or
irrational as legitimate starting points for design, and also the sense
that we should be challenging people to reassess their perceptions
and expectations. Established ideas should be jolted. Disruption
is the essence of effective communication

Postmodernism has reviewed the single-minded, utilitarian focus
of modernism and opened up design to a much broader range of influences.
The goal has been to make things that are designed more meaningful,
beyond just their functional and rational reason for being

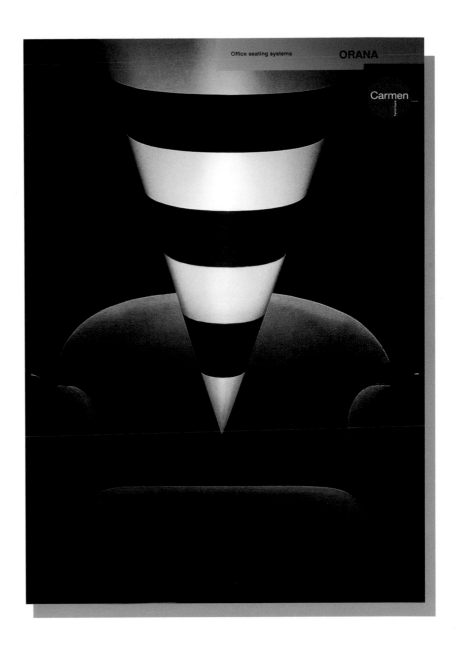

Sometimes the definition between what is a sign and what is an object
is deliberately blurred. A series of whimsical three-dimensional objects was
designed to promote an open day event at the Carmen Furniture showroom
temporary objects that signal a place of modernism and design,
and also function as drink stands and dispensers for packaged foods

Ephemeral

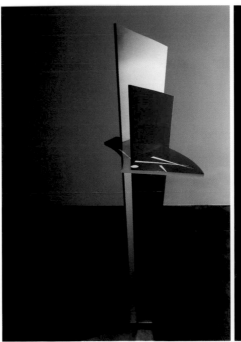

SPEC
TRO

Visual identity and details
from a brochure promoting
a printing company

SPECTRO

1994

TIDAL PRODUCTIONS: ACN 814367898 PO BOX 2074 WANTELME1 ROAD UPD 3145, MELBOURNE AUSTRALIA TELEPHONE 613 9822 9823 FACSIMILE 613 9821 0842 MOBILE 040803 18875, wallendarbvtile@bigpond.com

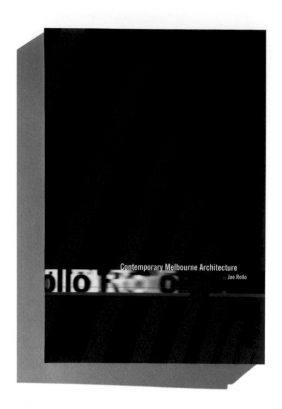

ROLLO COMMUNICATIONS
BLIGH VOLLER NIELD ARCHITECTS
GOLLINGS PHOTOGRAPHY

1999
1998
1992

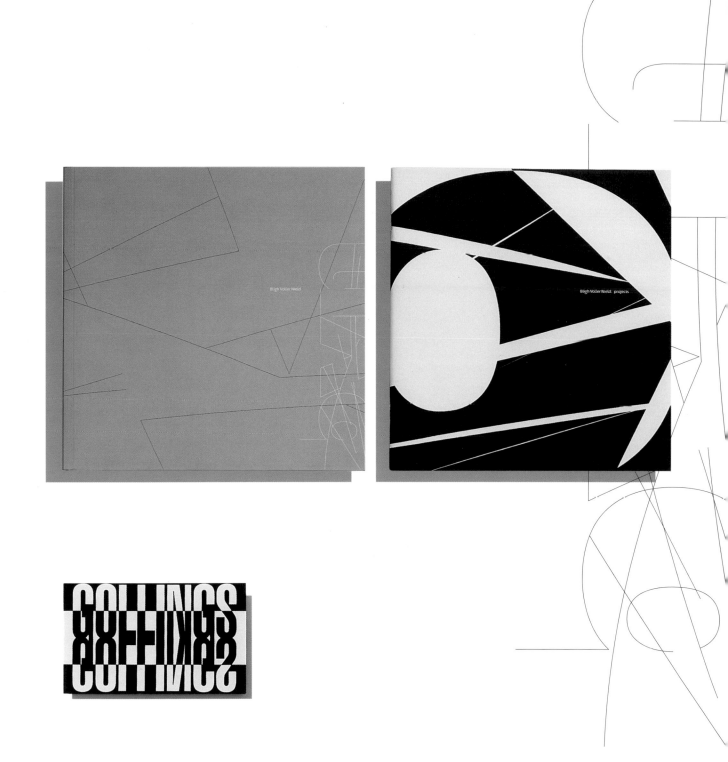

Gollings Photography: 1996 Annual Award, Tokyo Typo Directors Club

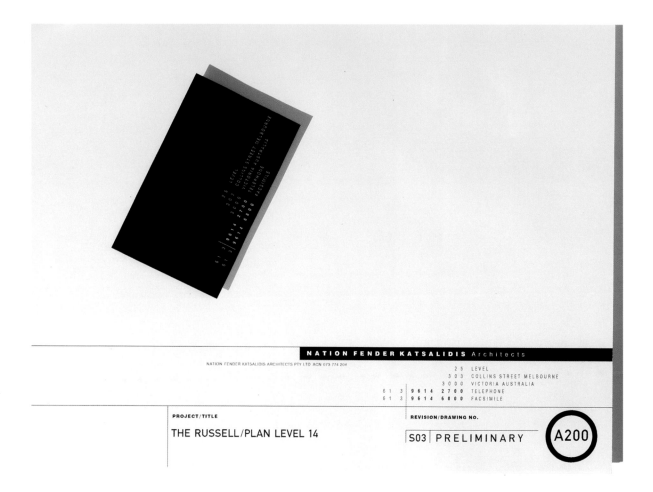

NATION FENDER KATSALIDIS Architects

NATION FENDER KATSALIDIS ARCHITECTS PTY LTD ACN 079 774 204

2 5   LEVEL
3 0 3   COLLINS STREET MELBOURNE
3 0 0 0   VICTORIA AUSTRALIA
61 3 9 6 1 4 2 7 0 0   TELEPHONE
61 3 9 6 1 4 6 8 0 0   FACSIMILE

PROJECT/TITLE

THE RUSSELL/PLAN LEVEL 14

REVISION/DRAWING NO.

S03 | PRELIMINARY   A200

NATION FENDER KATSALIDIS Architects

2 5   LEVEL
3 0 3   COLLINS STREET MELBOURNE
3 0 0 0   VICTORIA AUSTRALIA
61 3 9 6 1 4 2 7 0 0   TELEPHONE
61 3 9 6 1 4 6 8 0 0   FACSIMILE

Directors   Karl Fender
            Nonda Katsalidis
            Bill Krotiris
            Robert Nation

THE LORENZON GROUP
DENTON CORKER MARSHALL ARCHITECTS

1999
1989 to 1999

ARTSPEC

1989

The palimpsest is a graphic form, its layering of successive inscriptions and graphic traces revealing evidence of different moments and unrelated fragments of information. The inherently deconstructive nature of the palimpsest prefigures the computer, which automatically layers and deconstructs graphic information. This poster was designed and executed by hand, before the introduction of computers to the studio, pre-empting a compositional technique that would become automatic and generalised

As you were aware, the whole project started as part of a discussion with Peter Haythornthwaite centred around generating some original, highly "graphic" posters for our design client's studios.
While I recognise that we have already imposed on you a great deal, I wonder if I can be cheeky and impose on you further. We would like to commission the four judges to design the elusive posters for us and release them as a series for our clients in the New Year (February 1989?). Since the purpose of the exercise is "corporate image" for Artspec, and not utilitarian, there would be a few restrictions. The proposed brief would be as follows:

1) To be printed (quantity 1300) on very high quality stock and suitable for framing.
2) Maximum sheet size is A1 (594 x 841mm; 23.4 x 33.1 inches) (No billboards please.)
3) Artspec, in it's logo typeface (black) must appear somewhere, on the poster as would Garry Emery, Melbourne, 1989.
Otherwise, the brief is open for pure, graphic designer indulgence. Once these have been printed we would, of course be happy to ship 50 - 100 copies to your office for your own use.

Artspec.

NO.3 IN A SERIES OF 4. GARRY EMERY, MELBOURNE, 1989

KATSALIDIS ARCHITECTS

1999

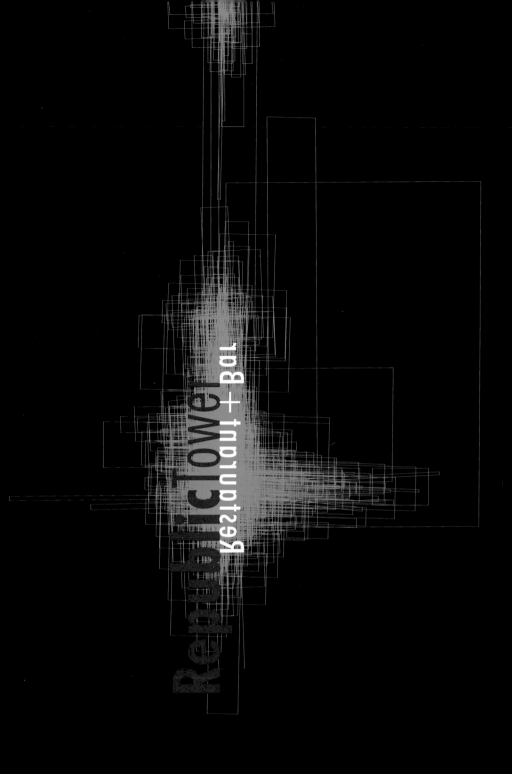

RepublicTower

Restaurant + Bar

Developing for the Future Australian Film Commission
Sydney.Brisbane.London

AUSTRALIAN FILM COMMISSION
EMERY VINCENT DESIGN

1999
1997

DEACONS GRAHAM & JAMES

award

ALEXANDER ZUBRYN

DAVID NOONAN

JOANNE CROKE

IAN FERGUSON

BRETT JONES AND SARAH STUBBS

Comforto 50
Comforto 50
mforto 50

invitation to the launch

WELL-APPOINTED, KEENLY PRICED, COMFORTO, THE NEW OFFICE CHAIR THAT MEANS BUSINESS.
YOU ARE INVITED TO THE LAUNCH OF THE COMFORTO RANGE OF OFFICE CHAIRS AT THE HAWORTH OMNI SHOWROOM
GROUND FLOOR, 395 COLLINS STREET, MELBOURNE 3000 6PM FRIDAY 19 SEPTEMBER 1997 RSVP: SANDRA HOSKINS BY THURSDAY 11 SEPTEMBER 1997 TELEPHONE 9629 5500 OR FACSIMILE 9629 5598

**THE IAN POTTER MUSEUM OF ART
HAYWORTH OMNI**

1999
1997

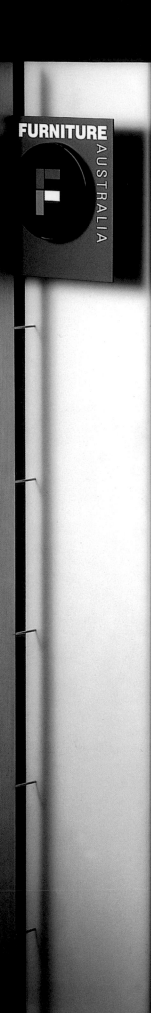

FURNITURE

Wilkhahn

FURNITURE AUSTRALIA

1995

Corporate office display for a mining company
Interior designers Carr Design Group

A hybrid work: informational, sculptural and interior fixture,
with both an aesthetic and an interpretive dimension

The nine metal cylindrical cores have decorative
etched images that tell a story about mining. The cylinders
themselves recall drilling cores

The traditional process of acid-etching printing blocks achieves
a distinctive effect on the aluminium cores

SANTOS, ADELAIDE

1998

TRANSURBAN CITYLINK, MELBOURNE

1997
1998

re reliable

Interior designers Carr Design Group

For a corporation that builds highways, we developed
images conveying a sense of speed. We configured them in a stretched-out
horizontal format that appears to float in the lobby of the corporate
headquarters. The taut yachting stays connote high-tech.
The installation has a spatial impact that transcends two-dimensionality

The company sells speed
and efficiency. For its highway
toll account operations
building, a graphic installation
dramatises some of the notable
landmarks of Melbourne's
newest road network

safer

Photographic image M&C Saatchi, Melbourne

JUST JEANS, MELBOURNE

1997

Interior designers Woods Bagot Architects

Overlay of graphics on a stripped
architectural aesthetic

Letters etched into frameless glass
balustrade functioning as identification,
minimalist decoration and elegant
safety marking

Clarity and impact using a limited
range of colours and materials

1998
Award of Excellence
Communication Arts
USA

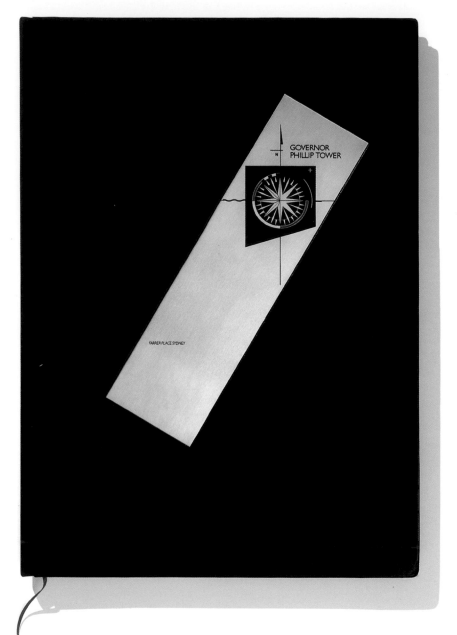

Acid-etched image on
a metal plate is incorporated
in the leather cover

A book to mark an office tower in
Sydney constructed on the historic location
of Australia's first Government House

Conveying a sense of history and the tactile
pleasures of materials and textures

GOVERNOR PHILLIP TOWER, SYDNEY

1991 to 1994

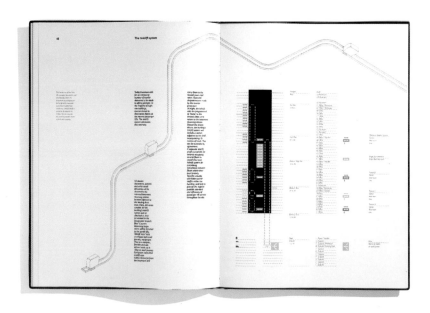

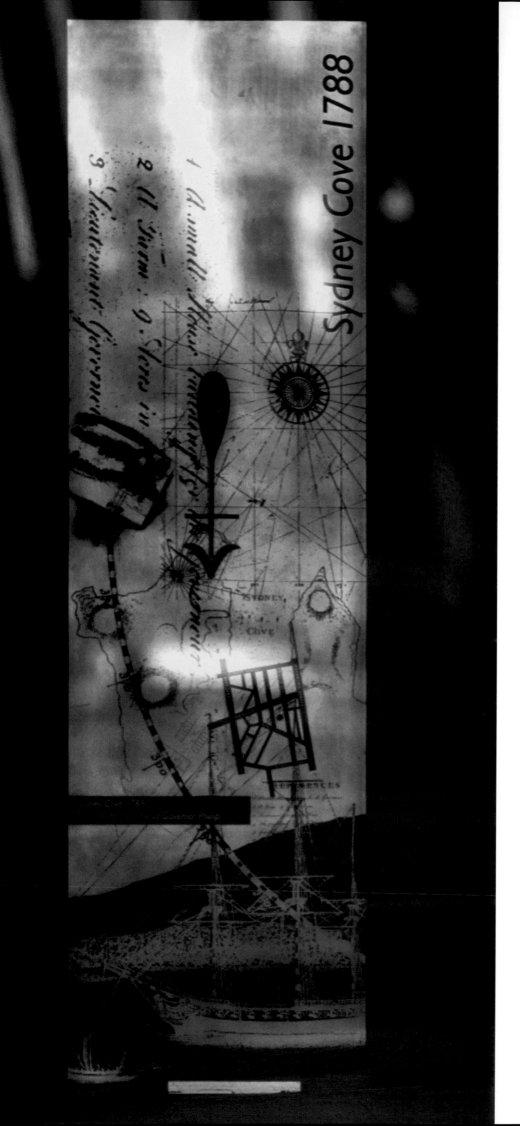

Sydney Cove 1788

The metal panels visible to pedestrians tell
the story of the location and development of this
significant site in the city. The layered images
are acid-etched, recalling traditional metal printing
plates and nautical instruments. Fragmentation
suggests the loss of the coherent whole,
an inevitable result of history

MARIAN HOSKING JEWELLER
SPACE FURNITURE

1998
1999

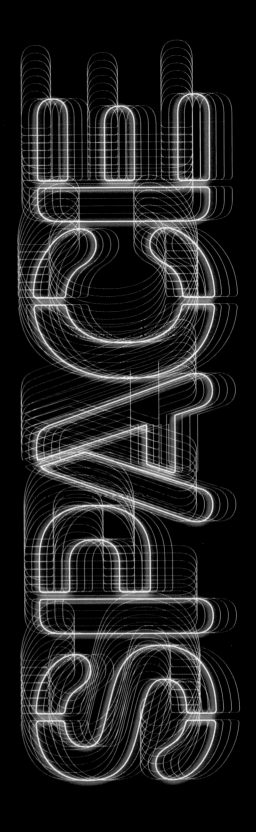

The constructivist
poster revisited invokes the
power of revolutionary
modernism as a framework
for presenting
contemporary designers

The cover is a visual pun on the idea of reproduction,
a contentious issue in craft, where the one-off object is
valued more than the serial or mass-produced

PRODUCTION REPRODUCTION JEWELLERY EXHIBITION
RMIT UNIVERSITY

1995
1994

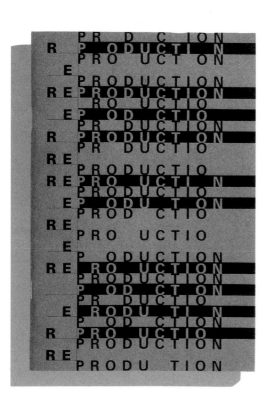

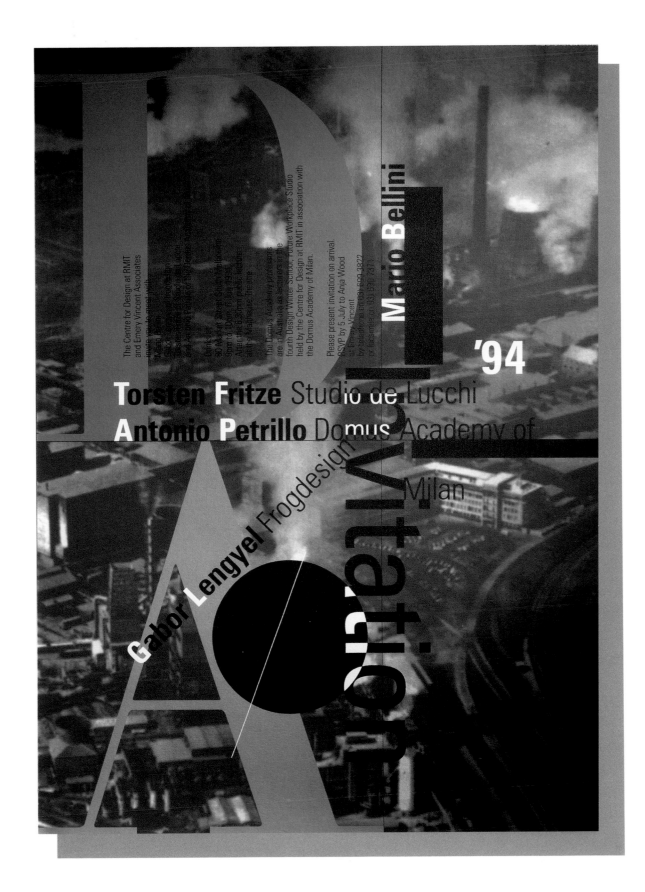

The Centre for Design at RMIT and Emery Vincent Associates invite you to an event with Mario Bellini

Date:
80 Market Street South Melbourne
9am to 10.30 6.00pm
After the 6.30am public lecture at the Malthouse Theatre

The Domus Academy professors are in Australia as lecturers in the fourth Design Winter School, Future Workplace Studio held by the Centre for Design at RMIT in association with the Domus Academy of Milan.

Please present invitation on arrival. RSVP by 5 July to Anja Wood at Emery Vincent by telephone at (03) 690 3822 or facsimile (03) 696 7571

Mario Bellini

'94

Torsten Fritze Studio de Lucchi
Antonio Petrillo Domus Academy of

Gabor Lengyel Frogdesign

Milan

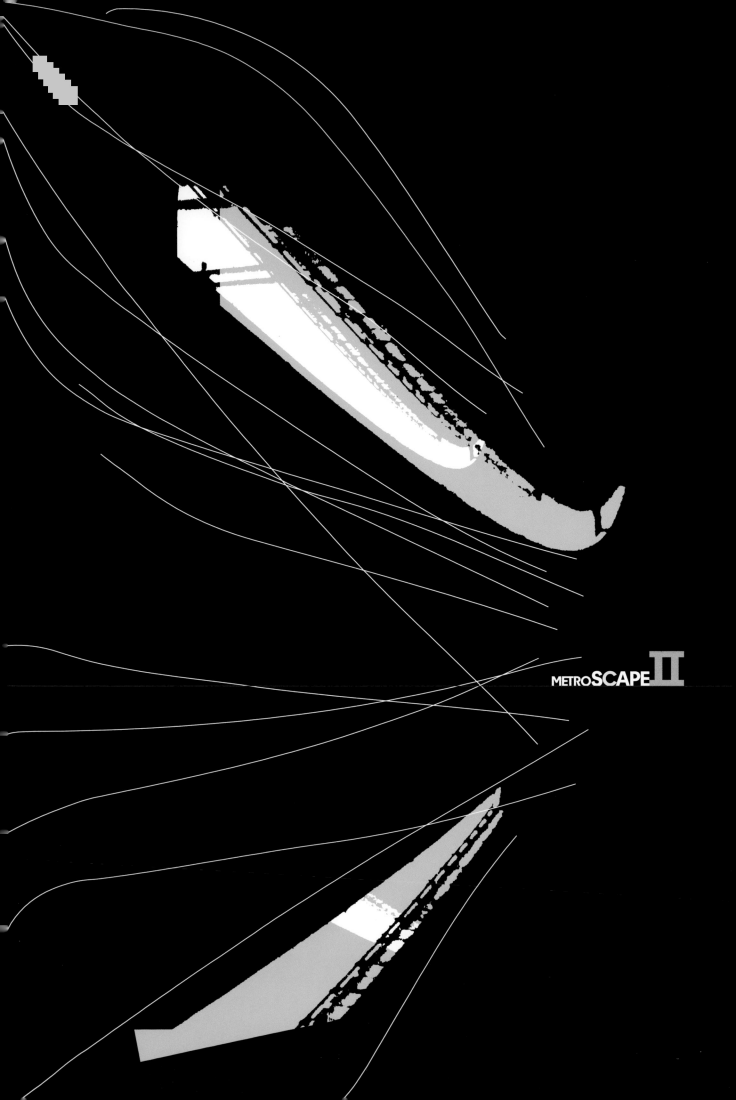

METRO**SCAPE** II

METROSCAPE II ART EXHIBITION
SINGAPORE EXHIBITION CENTRE

1996
1997

UME magazine
designed in collaboration
with Charlie Williams

UME
AUSTRALIAN FILM COMMISSION

1996 to 1999
1997

MELBOURNE INTERNATIONAL BIENNIAL

1999

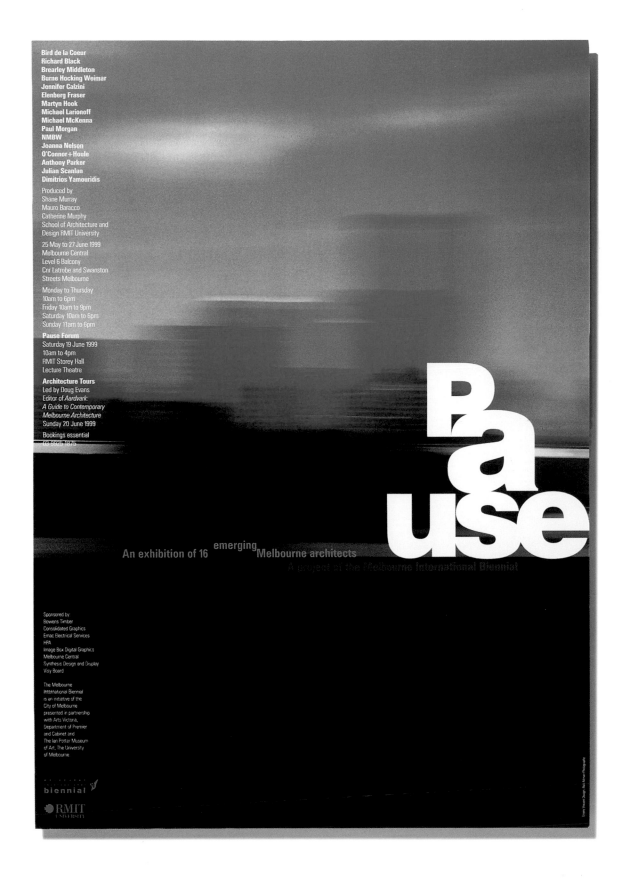

Bird de la Coeur
Richard Black
Brearley Middleton
Burne Hocking Weimar
Jennifer Calzini
Elenberg Fraser
Martyn Hook
Michael Larionoff
Michael McKenna
Paul Morgan
NMBW
Joanna Nelson
O'Connor+Houle
Anthony Parker
Julian Scanlan
Dimitrios Yamouridis

Produced by
Shane Murray
Mauro Baracco
Catherine Murphy
School of Architecture and
Design RMIT University

25 May to 27 June 1999
Melbourne Central
Level 6 Balcony
Cnr Latrobe and Swanston
Streets Melbourne

Monday to Thursday
10am to 6pm
Friday 10am to 9pm
Saturday 10am to 6pm
Sunday 11am to 6pm

Pause Forum
Saturday 19 June 1999
10am to 4pm
RMIT Storey Hall
Lecture Theatre

Architecture Tours
Led by Doug Evans
Editor of *Aardvark:
A Guide to Contemporary
Melbourne Architecture*
Sunday 20 June 1999
Bookings essential

**Pa
use**

An exhibition of 16 emerging Melbourne architects
A project of the Melbourne International Biennial

Sponsored by:
Bowens Timber
Consolidated Graphics
Emac Electrical Services
HPA
Image Box Digital Graphics
Melbourne Central
Synthesis Design and Display
Visy Board

The Melbourne
International Biennial
is an initiative of the
City of Melbourne
presented in partnership
with Arts Victoria,
Department of Premier
and Cabinet and
The Ian Potter Museum
of Art, The University
of Melbourne.

biennial

RMIT
UNIVERSITY

Orbit

MAGAZINE FOR INDUSTRIAL DESIGN

THE ECONOMIC VALUE OF DESIGN

DESIGN MANAGEMENT, AN UNDERGRADUATE PERSPECTIVE

IN WITH A NEW BROOM

5

RMIT University Faculty of the Constructed Environment School of Architecture+Design.
City Campus GPO Box 246V Melbourne 3001 Victoria Australia

Colour is the elusive element in design of products for everyday use, vulnerable to subjective interference than the other compliments of a design – form, materials and technology. The psychology component of colour plays a vital part in the succes of products in the marketplace and in the resolution of spaces for human environment. This issue examines some of the conditions in these areas from the viewpoint of the designer.

RMIT UNIVERSITY

1999

RMIT UNIVERSITY
AUSTRALIAN CONSTRUCTORS ASSOCIATION

1998
1998

OBJECTIVES

To require the highest standards
of skill, integrity and responsibility
of member companies.

To ensure that the ACA takes
a leading role in furthering the
reform and development of
the industry.

To provide an authoritative
and representative voice for major
construction contractors
on matters of common interest.

To enhance and promote the
status of construction contractors
and the industry which they serve.

To participate in the development
of relevant government policy and
influence decision making
concerning construction industry
issues.

To promote and support
improvements, by way of
standardisation, efficiency and
simplification in relevant laws
and regulations.

To facilitate the exchange of
technical information and
encourage further research on
technical and economic matters
of interest to construction
contractors.

01

OUR MISSION

The Australian Constructors Association (ACA) is dedicated to making
the construction industry more efficient, more competitive and better
able to contribute to the development of Australia through positive
leadership, open communication and a commitment to infrastructure.

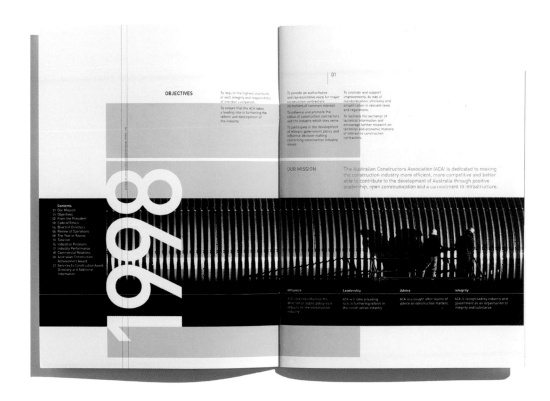

Contents

1998

Influence
ACA seeks to influence the
direction of public policy as it
impacts on the construction
industry.

Leadership
ACA will take a leading
role in furthering reform in
the construction industry.

Advice
ACA is a sought after source of
advice on construction matters.

Integrity
ACA is recognised by industry and
government as an organisation of
integrity and substance.

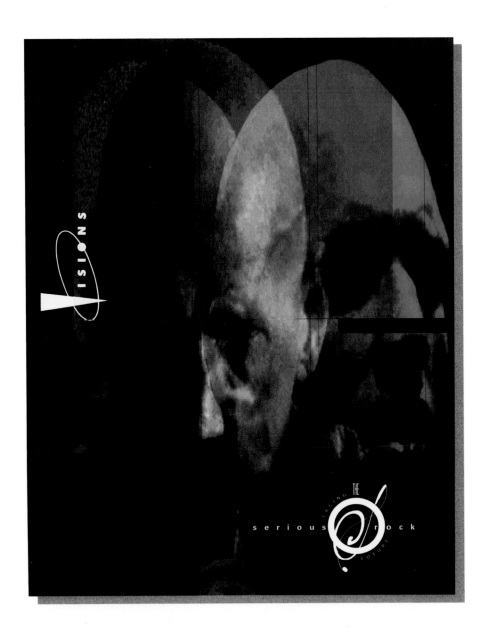

DesignInc

Architecture Urban Design Interiors

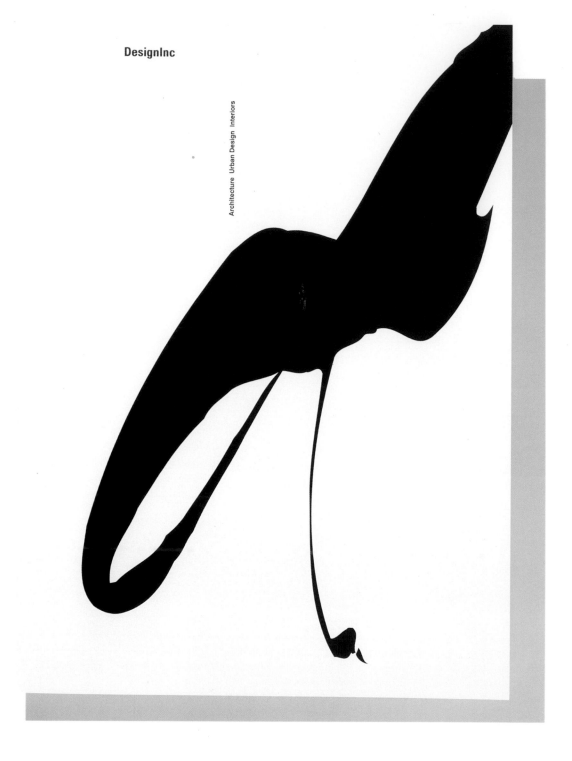

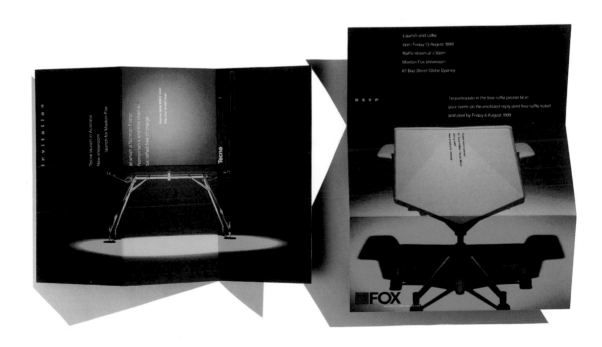

edible

architecture

ACCA

AN EXHIBITION
OF EDIBLE ARCHITECTURE
BY PROMINENT
AUSTRALIAN ARCHITECTS
7.30PM 23 OCTOBER 1997
AUSTRALIAN CENTRE FOR
CONTEMPORARY ART
DALLAS BROOKS DRIVE
SOUTH YARRA
VICTORIA AUSTRALIA

AUSTRALIAN CENTRE FOR CONTEMPORARY ART
AUSTRALIA GOLD EXHIBITION

1994
1993

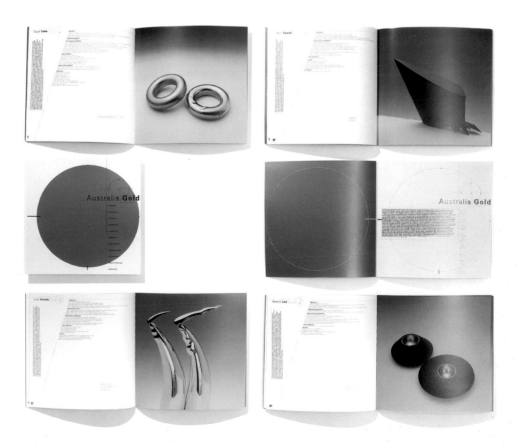

Emery Vincent Design is responsible for the exhibition concept, design and realisation. This includes the filming of dramatised sequences, the lighting concept, the design and manufacture of the exhibition infrastructure, and overall project management including the outsourced script development and curatorial and acting services

Exhibitions are typically object-based

Theatrical evocation is an alternative approach to presenting history, directly engaging the imagination and senses, and bypassing the need to intellectualise in order to 'experience' the past. Such evocation makes a subjective appeal rather than a rational one, immersing the viewers in the immediate realm of the senses where the imagination is fully activated and engaged. It is this approach that informs the exhibition 'Built on Gold: Victoria's gold journey and legacy, 1852 to 1862'

Sub-consultants
Building restoration Bates Smart
Lighting design Barry Webb Associates
Interpretation Look Ear
Audio design Sound Environment
Research Old Treasury Museum

There are no objects on view save for the actual scene itself in which the exhibition
is experienced – the historic gold vaults of the Old Treasury Museum. In this exhibition
the viewer is placed at the centre and not as a detached observer. As with radio,
the space of action, the characters and the atmosphere of the stories are summoned
inside the head: each viewer creates his or her own vision of the scene. This is an
active, dynamic engagement with history

BUILT ON GOLD EXHIBITION: OLD TREASURY MUSEUM, MELBOURNE

1998

Design is structure.
It is the thoughtful structuring
of elements in relation to
each other in order to transmit,
elicit, evoke, or in some
other way communicate an
idea or message

Four-dimensional design represents the new frontier for graphic designers.
As soon as you start to think of using electronic imagery, you have to
deal with time as a design component. We are intrigued by the idea of time
and what happens when you add time into the mix of design ingredients.
How you can use time creatively? What does it allow you to say?

EXHIBITION

INSTALLATION

DISPLAY

CONTAINER

The 2.4m cube is an exhibition installation/display unit/container designed for an exhibition of Emery Vincent Design's work. The articulated box splits into two elements, each with various facets hinged together. These two elements unravel in a dynamic linear configuration to form two distinctive topographies occuping the exhibition space. These topographies provide surfaces on which two-dimensional and three-dimensional material is displayed.

The cube is derived from the Chinese tangram, a two-dimensional puzzle based on a segmented square. The cube's absolute platonic simplicity is in contrast to the formal complexity of its fragmented constituents.

Viewing, touching and moving around the complex display unit and engaging in its formal and spatial games constitute part of the exhibition experience. The elegant metal unit sets the stage for the design work on display and becomes an iconic signature for Emery Vincent Design.

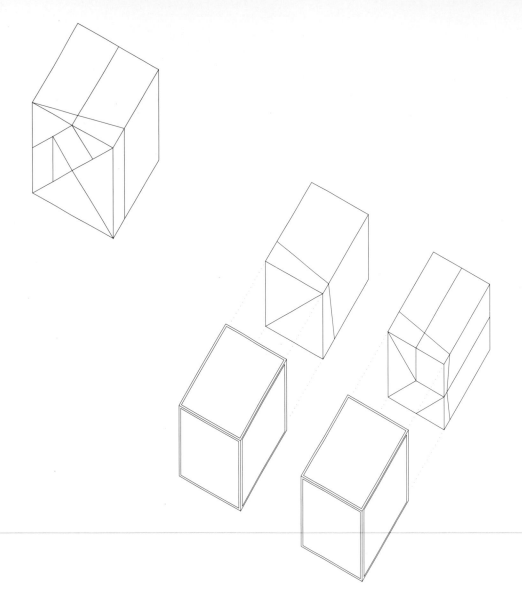

Elevation   Plan
                    The cube deconstructs into installations
                    of different scales and configurations

A corporate display that functions
as a spatial installation

Interior designers Inarc

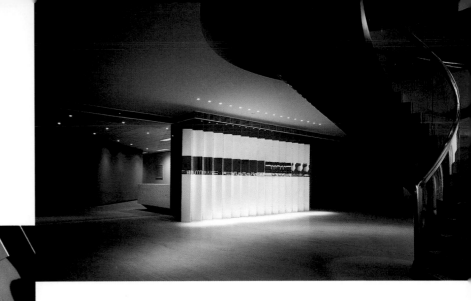

AMCOR, MELBOURNE

1993

Viewed from one direction, the slats line up to reveal a
contemporary corporate message. From the other direction,
they display references to company history. Straight on,
the images merge into a decorative abstract composition

Graphic design provides a bridge between identity, marketing and the built environment

Design concept
Abstract installation in the retail space
of Cathay City Complex for Cathay Pacific

CATHAY PACIFIC, HONG KONG

1998

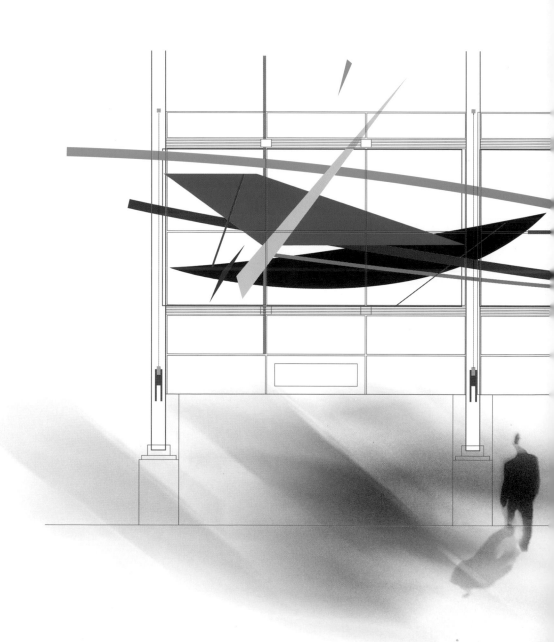

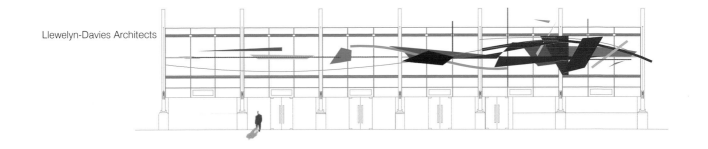

Llewelyn-Davies Architects

Subversion
The technical processes of design
are disclosed and incorporated into
the final image, throwing into
question expectations of completion

EMERY VINCENT DESIGN

1981

I am always looking for new ways of saying the same thing

Isamu Noguchi
Space of Akari and Stone
Chronicle Books
San Francisco, 1985, p9

Some projects from the past –
one or two going back nearly
thirty-five years – reflect
a disparate range of design
concerns and influences:
the rationalism of 1960s Swiss
modernism, the irrationalism
of dada and surrealism,
homages to constructivism
and futurism. These are
long-term design themes and
preoccupations that we
constantly revisit and
reinterpret – most recently
in light of the design
possibilities presented by new
media and technology

Industrial Safety Services
Designed by Whaite & Emery

1967

Garry Emery

Baker Institute
Designed by Whaite & Emery

1965

Paul Vincent

Penny Bowring

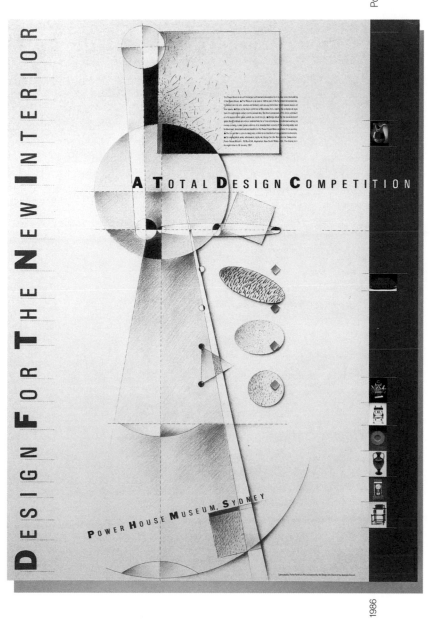

A TOTAL DESIGN COMPETITION

POWER HOUSE MUSEUM, SYDNEY

1986

MARCEL DUCHAMP

1985

Ken Stanley

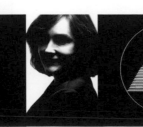

Royal Australian Institute of Landscape Architects

Pam Kimball

Jane Mooney

1980

Ray Parslow

Carlo Giannasca

Caffé e Cucina

1992

Australia Post at Expo 88

1988

Glaxo Australia

1976

Carole Drysdale

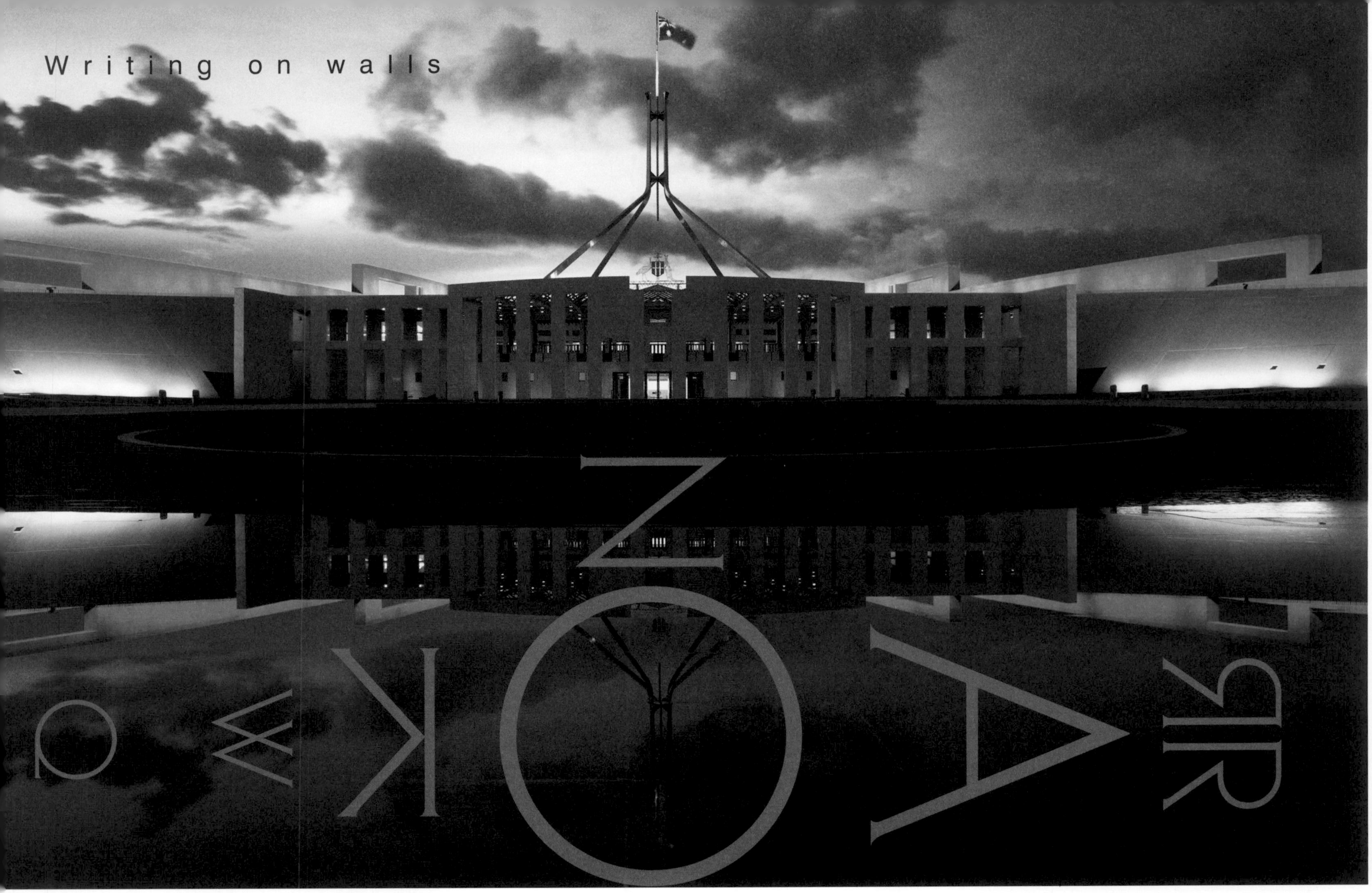
Writing on walls

Prof Haig Beck
Jackie Cooper

MONUMENT

Parliament House in Canberra – designed by Mitchell Giurgola Thorp and built in 1988 – is Australia's most significant monument since the War Memorial, with which it conducts a symbolic axial dialogue across the capital. A desire to write boldly on this building is integral to the monumental tradition. Where better to inscribe the marks of national confidence?

An extraordinary commission was issued to implement the collective cultural will to inscribe the stones of Parliament House: to design a new letterform for the building, specifically suited to incision and casting – the processes of architectural inscription. This was extraordinary because there had been no development of new letterforms for inscription since Roman times. The classical carved letters that attained an aesthetic pinnacle with the forms inscribed on the base of Trajan's Column in 113AD had never been superseded. The balance and beauty of Roman lapidary letters have satisfied different cultures, conditions and eras, with modifications, perhaps, but there has never been a decisive intention to develop new letterforms.

CONTEMPORARY

The logic of designing a new alphabet for Parliament House stems from several impulses. The building itself constituted the most compelling reason. Its design is predicated on a commitment to draw upon cultural memory without replication of historical forms. Familiarity might be invoked, but not in order to recreate the past. The architectural references are abstracted and indelibly stamped with contemporaneity. They engage memory to inform the present – and future – of its connective, formative and abiding relationship with the past. There was also the sense that it would be incongruent to impose on this new, nationally significant building the time-worn forms – however elegant – of an antique society. Just as Parliament House has reinterpreted enduring classical architectural values in light of its modern context and epoch, so too its inscriptions might express the local qualities of place – indeed, might express an authentic accent of Australia.

IDENTITY

The issue of national identity assumed a central prominence in the design of Parliament House. Yet there was no attempt to make an overtly 'Australian' building; no crude equation of vernacular imagery with national identity; no architectural version of Akubra hats and elastic-sided boots. Instead, the design incorporates certain qualities and attitudes that are discernibly Australian: light-filled expansive spaces, abundant use of native timbers and stone, straightforward detailing and decoration, tones of red and green (the traditional colours of the Senate and House of Representatives) that are taken from an Australian colour spectrum of the land, and even the terracotta tiles of suburbia to clad the peaked roofs of the two houses. These design gestures are not obviously drawn. They are carefully gauged metaphors expressing an Australian identity pervading a building that belongs to the wider, general culture of architecture.

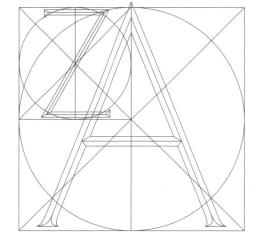

STEM

SERIFS

REFERENCES

The references to architecture's wider history are not direct quotations: they are abstracted. The building's stripped and sober elements evoke classical architectural traditions that recall democracy's origins and the nobility of Europe's civilisation. But these forms also simultaneously reveal the modernist ethos of a rational architecture cleansed of extraneous decoration and frankly expressive of its machine-crafted and mass-produced construction techniques. Both sets of associations are appropriate: the links with Europe and its humanistic cultural heritage, and engagement with the prevailing philosophical thrust of the twentieth century. Each explains something about the nation that Australia has become. The architects melded these references and associations with the evocations of place that are felt throughout the building. It is the land itself that is being conjured up by the materials and colours, light and space, and in the art and craft works that embellish the building. Parliament House is a building, but it is also the land, specifically a hill. It emerges half-buried from its site. The incomplete quality of Parliament House, as though the building at some later time would fill out Capital Hill and assert itself over the land, indicates the essential hesitation that is felt in declaring an Australian identity. This cannot be a simple matter, with the relatively small, disparate population still bonding into a national entity, hugging the extremities of a vast continent. The land is a constant datum, timeless and prevailing; a source of aesthetic and psychological nourishment. It is also the special province and refuge of Aboriginal people, whose presence in Parliament House is also acknowledged in references to the land.

CLASSICISM

The new alphabet for Parliament House was developed by Emery Vincent Design. The design process entailed considerable cultural and technical research. Like the design of the building, this research centred on issues of a national identity and a larger discourse of cultural traditions. In designing the new alphabet it was important to investigate the same sources that Romaldo Giurgola had explored in designing Parliament House. The lettering must resonate with the spirit and intentions of the architecture. Typography and architecture are different cultural artifacts yet identical in their purpose and design integrity.

Classicism is a significant cultural touchstone of architecture and letterforms alike. Western lettering ripened under the guiding hands of the Romans. Ever since, their sophisticated letters have conveyed clarity, substance and elegance. These qualities, admired and sought by the architects of Parliament House through its abstracted classical references, were similarly desired of the inscriptions that are to adorn the building. Garry Emery writes of his brief: 'The essence of the design approach for the letterforms is extracted from the classic/contemporary architecture of Romaldo Giurgola's new Parliament House and the requirements that messages should be capable of being incised into stone, cast into bronze or epoxy, etched into glass, or printed.'

PROCESS

The critical design constraint was the necessity for letterforms to be incised into marble and granite.

This was the essential technical touchstone of the design development. It required going back to first principles, analysing the origins, design structure and production techniques of Greek and Roman lapidary letters. (Emery Vincent also reviewed print-based letterforms to inform the design of the extensive and varied signage system needed for the building.) The universally admired qualities of Roman lapidary letterforms derive from an aesthetic that is intrinsic to their manner of production. The grace of calligraphic motion suffuses the underlying structure of geometric proportions and the incised technical precision of the letterforms. Outlines of characters were first traced onto the stone, then chiselled. This technique embodies the act of writing, retaining the touch of the hand moving to produce sweeping forms with variable line thickness as greater pressure bears on the downstrokes. Serifs, the inflections at the ends of incised letters, developed naturally from this fabrication method. They are a technical response to the need to finish off chiselled letters without splintering the stone. They also answer an aesthetic need to prevent upright strokes from seeming to swell slightly at the centre. (Entasis, an optical illusion, was also confronted by the architects of classical Greece, who devised tactics for overcoming the apparent visual distortion in the design of their temples.)

TYPOGRAPHY

In its subsequent historical developments, lettering diverged from its partnership with architecture.

The collapse of classical civilisation meant the demise of classical values and cultural forms, and the abandonment of monumental inscription. European letterforms then pursued a different trajectory – the 'painterly' mode of calligraphy, which was to introduce lower case characters (minuscules) to the upper case antique alphabet. Distinctive regional styles also flourished. Letterforms changed with new writing habits and techniques. Paper 'replaced parchment and vellum. Printing, devised in the mid-fifteenth century, was the most significant technical event in the development of lettering. Printed type, at first closely modelled on handwritten characters, gained acceptance by replicating the culturally familiar forms of the time. Gradually typography displaced calligraphy and came to dominate the development of letterforms. Type responded to its own technical constraints and created its own formats. Traces of earlier letterforms have persisted in type forms: for instance, serifs, which recall classical techniques of inscription; flourishes originating in calligraphy; and italic faces that mimic handwritten script.

CLASSICAL

The classical world was not to be forgotten. By the mid-fifteenth century, the Renaissance movement on the Italian peninsula was substantially refocusing Europe towards a glorious classical heritage. It rediscovered classical proportioning systems that expressed the new humanist ideals current in architecture and painting, and reinterpreted the ancient cultural traditions brimming with newly-found significance: the 'cult of the Antique', as Pevsner termed it. The Renaissance built monuments of balance and clarity for the princes of state and church, a highly cultured, hugely aggressive patrician class steeped in financial and political acumen. Such patrons had a keen appetite for inscriptions, and indeed, inscriptions had been integral to the antique classical tradition they were pleased to invoke. Rediscovered Roman letterforms were found to be perfectly suited to the new cultural mood of rebirth. Other cultural movements supplanted the Renaissance. From the latter eighteenth century, a classical revival swept Europe and reached distant places like the United States and Australia. Grand monuments invoking the forms of Greece and Rome were built: temples, pantheons, rotundas, palaces. This neoclassical momentum was sustained – in ever more elaborate guises – through the nineteenth century, and was only finally exhausted following World War I when the rise of modernism signalled the end of the old order.

The revival of Roman lapidary letterforms accompanied each new enthusiasm for classical architecture. Monuments in Berlin, Vienna and Washington were inscribed in elegant classical letters – and quite deliberately so, for their use implies by association that the characteristics of such a splendid imperial power somehow reflected on these distant cultural progeny. The extent of the impact of Roman lapidary letterforms can be appreciated by observing how Hitler and Mussolini, New Deal America and Stalinist Russia all used the same lettering to inscribe their most significant monuments. All invoked the antique classical letters perfected on the base of Trajan's Column to validate their epochs.

ENDURING

The letterforms of Roman inscriptions have not been superseded in nearly 2000 years because whenever there was a need to inscribe monuments, these letters answered all the requirements of dignity, balance and decorum. Roman letterforms did experience modifications in the centuries following the Renaissance as journeymen carvers, completely estranged from the motivating force of Roman culture, struggled to copy the perfected classical forms. Their rustic efforts can be seen on many tombstones as earnest but debased versions of classical rigour.

REGIONAL

The provenance of the new letterforms for Parliament House was to be classical. Yet transformation of the antique model was important because a sense of modernity, and perhaps regional identity too, was sought. Emery Vincent Design's graphic study of letterforms reviewed the history of Australian examples. Country signs and city advertising, labels, posters, playbills and newspapers indicated a regional spirit. The study discerned such recurring characteristics as the 'notional' serifs appearing on sans serif faces, or upstrokes and downstrokes with the same line thickness. These gave clues for combining the abstracted distinctive elements of regional letterforms with abstracted interpretations of Roman lapidary letters to produce the new alphabet for Parliament House. Garry Emery explains: 'The proportions of the characters refer to classic Roman lapidary letters. Other distinctive characteristics are derived from letterforms crudely hand-painted onto Australian vernacular buildings – these being the oblique letter endings to the characters C, G, J and S and the "notional" radiused serif, left as a calligraphic gesture from the signwriter's paint-loaded brush. Equally weighted upstrokes and downstrokes produce messages of graceful and distinctive visual form with even colour.'

MESSAGE

What is to be inscribed on the stones of Parliament House? This is not a simple question because it defines a hiatus in the perception of a national identity. Actually there is no inscription yet planned, beyond simply naming 'AUSTRALIA'. The project to select a suitable message has so far not generated any confident consensus. This is not a failure of nerve: it is a straightforward reading of the current condition. The architecture itself seems empty, incomplete. This is expressed in the way the main facade is organised as an open screen with the flag-mast above delineating the frame of the building, in fact defining a void. Parliament House is a monument awaiting completion. Its walls are awaiting inscriptions. And Australia is still attempting to fill out a plausible national vision. There has been questioning about who Australians are, where they are going, their relationship to the land and its original people. The quest for cultural identity is compulsively pursued and must lead inexorably towards revaluation of the innocent pastoral myth that has always warmed and united Australians. The nation now needs a more mature, rounded reflection of itself. Maturity depends on facing up to contradictions and agonies: the displacement of the original owners of the land, the continuing desecration of its frail surface, and exploitation of its resources.

Australia's identity has been heavily imprinted by tragedy – the traumas of convict banishment, the dogged sacrifices of pioneers, and the grim heroics of war. These humiliations and defeats have given Australia its cast of national heroes: the laconic drover, the little Aussie battler, the digger. But national identity is also a living organism exposed to changing perceptions. Australia has grown accustomed to seeing itself myopically in terms of golden days and good times, but it is now necessary to broaden the references of national identity to include other vital tragedies in Australia's history: the European decimation of Aboriginal culture and the social marginalisation of non-European citizens. Perhaps the present inability to inscribe this monument is the most eloquent message. In time, a positive message will be formulated and inscribed onto Parliament House. In addition to spelling out its meaning, the handsome letterforms will express their harmonious relationship with the design philosophy of the building, and also convey the distinctive accent of Australia.

Once graphic design relocates itself from the printed page and escapes the corporate desk, the coffee table and the hyper zone of the electronic media and goes out into the built environment, it must conduct a new dialogue with a different set of dynamics. This new dialogue is with pedestrians, traffic, public space, architecture, hard and soft landscaping, building and town planning regulations, noise, weather and the aggression of construction sites. Environmental graphic design is a very public design form. Here graphics is not simply a container for communicating information – it takes

on the significant role of defining
and ordering urban space. Graphics
has a major impact on people's
everyday surroundings – signs are
everywhere – and consequently there
is great responsibility on designers
to lead in creating legibility and clarity
in the urban environment

It is important for the designer
to have a sense of time and place
and to recognise when to

turn the volume up

and when to turn it down

When enough design is too much

Garry Emery

DISORDER

Twenty or thirty years ago, designers confidently assumed that their task was to bring as much of the city as possible under their control. We are no longer so sure about this. We suspect that it is actually possible to overdesign the city. Cities need order at many levels, from fundamental urban planning guidelines through to signage and street lighting. Safety and clarity are essential to allow citizens to walk confidently in streets and enjoy a range of different urban experiences, day time and night time. But comprehensive demands for order and control tend to suppress the urban disorder that spontaneously arises in cities. Often that disorder is what makes a place tick: disorder is the reason people gravitate to Times Square or Piccadilly Circus, especially at night. Disorder gives Hong Kong or Tokyo a special energy that would be stifled if prescriptive legislated design criteria were introduced to those cities. Some places are better for having no design controls, or at least only controls that allow urban intensity to flourish and find its own limits.

AUTHENTICITY

The retrogressive urban vision presented in the futuristic movie *Blade Runner* (1982) is dark and menacing. It is a cautionary warning of how cities could degenerate into stratified canyons, the lowest levels dripping with black rain, and anarchy rife in the streets. Yet because of its intensity and raw atmospheric power, *Blade Runner* also presents a compelling vision: at least this is a place with a strong identity and a dynamic pulse. So often we are located in urban or suburban areas drained of energy and a sense of place, areas that have legibility perhaps but no spirit or authenticity. The brutality of the *Blade Runner* urban paradigm is unacceptable. But before dismissing this urban aesthetic out of hand, it offers some insights: chaos isn't necessarily bad. Complexity and disorder are often positive forces generating energy and identity. Confusion has its own fascination and value. The layering of different styles and eras and the build-up of detritus from the past do not necessarily have to be torn down and cleaned up.

PARIS

If the great modernist architect, Le Corbusier, had got his way in the 1930s, he would have wiped clean half of Paris in the name of increasing people's access to healthy sunshine. Yet what everyone loves about Paris is the intimacy of its medieval street patterns and the disorder and surprise of its urban plan. This urban untidiness is aesthetically and psychologically satisfying. Even great designers can be blind to the real value of what exists around them, and even the best and most rational of motives do not always result in the most desirable outcomes. Since the early 1970s there has been a basic shift in the way we are able to view cities. It is no longer appropriate to imagine that we can impose a definitive ordering system, or use a blanket design methodology throughout the city. Not only are cities bigger than they have ever been. A powerful new culture has also developed: the culture of pluralism.

Night Cities Workshop 1999
Massachusetts Institute of Technology
Boston

MEGALOPOLIS

Many cities over the past thirty years have blown out into megalopolises. London and Los Angeles spread forever. Both Sydney and Brisbane now extend for a couple of hundred kilometres up and down the Australian coast. Where is the city? What bits do we try and order through design? What degree of impact can we expect design to have? Not only are we now dealing with the huge size of cities; we are also dealing with a culture of pluralism where there are lots of competing ideologies and different viewpoints, all of them as valid (or not) as each other. The point about a culture of pluralism is that there is no longer a single dominant ethos that everyone subscribes to: there is no one right way of doing things. So we have unwieldy urban megalopolises and proliferating cultural pluralism. How can we tie things together?

COMPLEXITY

Cities are built on complexity and disorder. They have always existed as melting pots, places where countless disparate things converge – different people, customs, ideas, artifacts, all mingled together. But this inherent tendency towards complexity has accelerated in the decades since the advent of television and cheaper international travel. Now our culture, wherever we live, has become international. Our populations are multicultural. These developments inevitably change our perceptions as designers. The city is too big for any single entity to grapple with. Another way of looking at it is to say that the city needs to be broken down into smaller precincts before we consider ways to tackle the issues of urban signage, lighting, legibility and safety.

VILLAGE

The city is a confederation of villages, each developing its own character, subtly different from its neighbouring districts. These different villages need different orders of legibility. In some parts of the city, we are strangers; and in other parts of the city that we habitually move through or live in, we are locals. The need for information and signage differs. The commercial business district, which attracts the most strangers and probably also contains most of the civic institutions, is a place where a high degree of legibility is needed. But other villages in the city develop their own intimate characters and local attractions. These places do not need much official intervention because people there either know the place as locals, or they are drawn there and will be prepared to explore the village and discover it for themselves. Urban legibility is a holy grail, but it is not required in all places to the same degree.

Urban legibility is often most threatened by urban planners who lay down disorienting road systems in which strangers could never locate themselves without extensive signage. In a grid city it is possible to follow your nose to find your way. It is also relatively easy to navigate a route in a city that intelligently follows the topography and uses the ridge roads and valley floors and river edges as obvious orientation devices. In most other places there is a need for extensive wayfinding signage. People moving around a city develop cognitive maps to locate themselves. They remember particular buildings, a tree on the corner, the blue house near the bus stop. Where there is little underlying order to the urban planning, the first responsibility of the designer of signage and lighting is to clarify the mental maps that people need to carry around in their heads. This task is not necessarily to clarify the urban space. It is only at specific destinations that signage and lighting can take on the other roles of celebrating place and shaping urban space.

GENIUS LOCI

Urban legibility is a critical issue for the site of the Sydney 2000 Olympic Games at Homebush Bay. The urban form is highly legible, with the central boulevard acting as a giant urban foyer to the various Olympic venues. The sheer volume of people attending major sporting and cultural events places great pressure on the signage. But over and above its function of providing efficient public information and wayfinding, the signage also needs to help establish an instant atmosphere, to signal that here is a special place of excitement and pleasure. It always takes a major effort to create such an effect on a big greenfield site. Yet it will be more the richness of the experiential qualities that will determine the success of Homebush Bay as an urban precinct, and not so much how legible it is.

Emery Vincent Design has been closely involved in the design of both the signage and the emblematic pylon structures. The striking Olympic Plaza pylons combine several roles. They give a monumental scale and identity to this significant civic space. They are orientation devices. They signal festivity. They contain services and information. And they offer people shade and directions. During the day the pylons and the grand boulevard define the urban spine and make the urban form of Homebush Bay evident. At night there are opportunities to paint the space through dramatic lighting. What is important is that the designers resist the temptation to do this with the typical coolness and control that designers generally bring to urban design. These spaces at night can be vibrant, complex, exciting, and not just 'well designed'.

CONTROL

A lot of what makes a city a desirable place is not under the control of designers. The civic domain is built by many forces, most of them unrelated to design, and that is what most people actually prefer. As designers, we should pace ourselves in terms of where we can make design statements in the city, and where it's better to step back and let other forces do the running.

1

Into the fourth dimension

Emery Vincent Design

MULTIPLE

Today's reader is also a television viewer and an Internet user, accustomed to absorbing the screen's multiple hybrid visual codes and instant bites of information. How does graphic design engage this reader/viewer? While two-dimensional graphics cannot deliver the sensational, fast-moving three-dimensionality of film, it does offer some visual approximation through graphic tactics based on fragmentation, disruption, deconstruction, collage and layering – all reflecting the disintegration and speed characteristic of modern society. But why limit graphic design to just two dimensions?

SPACE

Designing for three dimensions is different from designing for the page. Many principles are the same – balance, order, composition. But the techniques are often quite different. In three-dimensional graphics, which includes signage and wayfinding, you can't just scale up a two-dimensional concept. You have to focus on a three-dimensional, spatial premise.

TIME

Something similar happens in four-dimensional design. Time is a completely new factor. You can't take a sequence of static two-dimensional images and match them with a soundtrack. The questions we ask here: How can you use time creatively? What does it allow you to say?

FRONTIER

Space-time design is the new frontier. Graphic design is now operating in three and four dimensions as well as the page-bound domain of two dimensions. As the influence of graphic design grows, film, video and animation are increasingly incorporated into our repertoire of design media. Meanwhile, the Internet is powering a communications revolution in terms of the way information is both sent and received. The Internet offers graphic design the most exciting challenge since Gutenberg invented moveable type in 1455: it's a vast print paradigm shift.

INTERNET

The range of communication on the Internet runs from marketing to pure information, from on-line shopping to banking, from the technical to the cultural to the bizarre. There are no limits to content. The Internet opens everything up. The Internet is very different from the static page. Graphic designers have yet to develop ways to exploit the potential methods for conveying information available on the Internet. But we are not confined to type and images anymore. The Internet provides space and also time. The Web operates in real time. The challenge for graphic designers is to use speed and motion – and also sound – as well as text and image. The page has become a dynamic, liquid field capable of infinite manipulation.

STAPLE

Two-dimensional print has been the staple of graphic design for six centuries. With the Internet, moving images are becoming the new staple of graphic design. In a real sense the graphic designer is becoming a movie director dealing with moving images – animation, film and other forms that have not yet been invented. Graphic design up until now has always been silent: the word on the page is mute. With the Internet that too changes, and the word may be spoken or sung or shouted. Sound becomes as important as sign.

READING

Reading on the Internet is not the linear experience that it is with a newspaper or book. We use the Internet in real time and we interact with it. The Internet allows us to engage with cyberspace on a one-to-one basis and navigate our own pathways through it. Graphic design is increasingly providing these pathways for a new kind of reading that is beginning to happen.

Following pages: Television images marketing Deakin University

▶

Prof Garry Emery, design director
Emery Vincent Design

I have never
seen the practice
as part of the
mainstream, nor
as part of the
avant garde, but
as occupying some
kind of curious
middle ground –
with a keen interest
in new wave
media and the
digital future. There
is no special
focus on two-,
three- or
four-dimensional
design, simply a
general interest in
each. Similarly,
there is an equal
commitment to
large, small and
middle-sized
projects, as well as
an interest in both
the cultural
and the commercial –
although to
every commercial
project we
endeavour to bring
a cultural
dimension. Our
design practice
happily occupies its
own territory

Since 1987
Marita Abdic
Imogen Ashlee
Diane Astone
Bridget Auld
Emma Barlow
Michael Barnes
Helen Barry
Domenico Bartolo
Kane Black
Vanessa Block
Kristen Bloink
Lara Bosse
Penelope Bowring
Ty Bukewitsch
Vanya Byak
Phil Campbell
Alessandro Capanna
Ariel Carthew
Noel Caulfield
Alexander Chalaby
Alvin Chan
Peter Chilton
Paul Clark
Ray Clarke
Janna Cochrane
Brett Coelho
Sarah Cope
David Crampton
Natalie Cuthbert
Laura Dalrymple
Ann Davey
Jeffrey Davey
Garth Davis
Rob Deutscher
Genevieve Dietrich
Gary Domoney
Job van Dort
Carole Drysdale
Jane Eaton

Tony Lee
James Lin
Stephanie Lindsay
John Lovett
Alan Marshall
Raine Marshall
Frans Martens
Celina McEwen
Jennifer McIntosh
Angela McMinn
Hilda Mendham
Jacques Meunier
Beth Milauskas
Prue Mitchell
Jane Mooney
Tony Morgan
Kim Moroney
Alan Morrison
Tim Murphy
Michelle Muter
Ian Newton
Andrea Nixon
Greg Olijnyk
Alison Orr
Ray Parslow
Ursula Pastrikas
Vijay Patel
Romy Pearce

With Emery Vincent Design for more than five years

Ty Bukewitsch Senior graphic designer and information technology manager

Alvin Chan Senior graphic designer

David Crampton Senior architectural designer and environmental graphics project manager

Andie Froutzis Senior graphic designer

Eva Lee Senior architectural designer and new media designer

Alison Orr Senior executive assistant

Linda Popovic Senior architectural designer

Anita Woo Graphic designer

Benedicte Ebbesen
Andrew van Embden
Joan Eway
Jeanette Fallon
Emma Fisher
Andrew Fowler-Brown
Carolyn Frank
Andie Froutzis
Natasha Galea
Helen Gasson
Paul Genney
Hans Gerber
Carlo Giannasca
Nada Gisonda
Caroline Goldsmith
Shannon Grant
Rosanne Green
Jessica Grinter
Ryan Guppy
Catherine Hall
Simon Hancock
Nancy Harlock
Trish Hart
Pam Hartmann
Carolyn Heffernan
Andrew Hogg
Trudi Hollis
Simon Hong
Deborah Hopkins
Kirsty Hough
Marion Huxley
Sue Isaacs
Lucy Isherwood
Anja Jacob
Mark Janetzki
Julia Jarvis
Lynette Jeffery
Georgina Jones
Stefan Kahn
Pelagia Kambouris
Damian Kelly
Pam Kimball
Ulla Korgaard
Dana Kornhauser
Margot Koudstall
Alexander Kranz
Maurice Lai
Jennie Landrigan
Eva Lee
Gini Lee

Melissa Pilgrim
James Poon
Linda Popovic
Sonia Post
Helen Prebble
Joanne Pritchard
Tanuja Puveendran
Mathew Quick
Jon Quinn
Tim Richardson
Vanessa Ryan
Verity Saunders
Oliver Schmoldt
Catherine Scott
Kate Scott
Jane Sinclair
Bilyana Smith
Graeme Smith
Karlie Smith
Lorinda Smith
Nino Soeradinata
Peter Squires
Andrew Stacey
Ken Stanley
Marion Steet
Anna Stephen
Marguerite Stinson
Hayley Tanner
Pete Tanpipat
Hsu-Li Teo
Shane Thomson
Marina Tores
Stephanie Valentin
Alison Vaughan
Marius Vogl
Sophie Waters
Brigitte Watson
Sally Watts
Adrian Weller
Kasper Wensveen
Thomas Wiebach
Peter Wilson
Anita Woo
Judy Worthington
Anna Zagala

PROFILE

Emery Vincent Design was established in Melbourne by Garry Emery and Paul Vincent in 1980. The Sydney studio, directed by Penelope Bowring, opened in 1987. This multidisciplinary practice of forty-five personnel – which includes graphic designers, architects, interior and new media designers – has core skills in graphic design, environmental and wayfinding graphics, corporate and brand identity, corporate communications, marketing planning, and project management. Most recently, the practice has begun pioneering space-time design for the Internet and digital media.

Emery Vincent Design is responsible for one of Australia's largest and most complex graphics commissions, Parliament House in Canberra, which included the design of a special new typeface, Parliament, for the building's monumental inscriptions.

Other major institutional, identity, signage and wayfinding commissions include the Australia Post corporate identity program; Australian embassies in Beijing and Tokyo; Australian National Maritime Museum, Sydney; Australian National War Memorial, Canberra; 'Built on Gold' exhibition at Melbourne's Old Treasury Building; Cathay Pacific International Headquarters; Hotel and Flight Training Centre, Hong Kong; Sydney's Cook and Phillip Park, Kuala Lumpur City Centre, Malaysia; Melbourne Exhibition Centre; Melbourne International Airport Terminal; Brisbane International Airport Terminal; Melbourne Museum; National Gallery of Victoria; the Powerhouse museum of applied arts and sciences, Sydney; Putrajaya Malaysia; Royal Melbourne Zoological Gardens; State Library of Victoria; Sydney Opera House; and a number of projects for the Sydney 2000 Olympics. These include the signage masterplan, Olympic Park railway station, Homebush Bay ferry terminal, Stadium Australia, Olympic Tennis Centre, Aquatic Centre, Athletic Centre, urban elements design manual, Olympic Boulevard implementation, streets and avenues implementation, plaza pylons signage, and the Sydney International Regatta Centre.

Garry Emery

Design director, member of
the Alliance Graphique
Internationale, Adjunct Professor
at Deakin University

Paul Vincent

Director specialising in
marketing and responsible for
finance and contract
administration. Before forming
Emery Vincent Design with
Garry Emery in 1980,
Paul Vincent was in marketing,
working with international
corporations Ciba-Geigy and
Glaxo Pharmaceuticals

Penny Bowring

Has directed the Sydney
studio since its establishment
in 1987. Penny Bowring has
led major environmental
graphics projects including the
Singapore Exhibition Centre,
Star City, Downing Centre
Law Courts, and Australian
National Maritime Museum, as
well as collaborating on
urban signage programs
for the Sydney 2000 Olympics
site at Homebush Bay,
Olympic Park railway station
and Stadium Australia

Books

Tony Lee, ed, *Building on Tradition*, Emery Vincent Associates, Melbourne, 1986

Garry Emery, *Emery Vincent Associates Selected Works*, Emery Vincent Associates, Melbourne, 1990

Who's Who in Graphic Design, Benteli-Werd Verlag, Zurich, 1994, p27

Garry Emery, *CI*, Emery Vincent Design, Melbourne, 1996

Garry Emery and Peter Steidl, *Corporate Image and Identity Strategies: Designing the Corporate Future*, Business & Professional Publishing, Sydney, 1997

Anna Bodi, Glenn Maggs and Don Edgar, Emery Vincent Design: I Just Wanted to Colour In, *When Too Much Change is Never Enough*, Business & Professional Publishing, Sydney, 1997, pp23–39

Garry Emery, *Idiom*, Emery Vincent Design, Melbourne, 1998

Magazine articles

Jeremy Press, 'Garry Emery, Another View', *Idea*, no 186, 1984, pp76–92

'Australian Design Now: Garry Emery', *Axis*, Winter 1989, pp98–99

'Emery Vincent Associates', *Communication Arts*, May/June 1991, pp88–99

'Whither the elephant and the kangaroo?', *Dialect: the official journal of the Design Institute of Australia*, Issue 3, April/June 1992, pp14–15

Marcus O'Donnell, 'Garry Emery: Looking backwards towards the future', *Monument*, no 6, 1995, pp18–23

Virginia Trioli, 'Emery Vincent: Shaking the Tree', *Graphis*, no 310, vol 53, July/August 1997, pp40–51

'Protectors of the Corporate Identity', *Business Review Weekly*, September 19, 1997, p115

'Three Australians: Ken Cato, Garry Emery, Barrie Tucker', exhibition catalogue, *The World of Graphic Design at the Galerie von Oertzen*, 1997, pp114–19

Garry Emery 'Degrees of Cool: Reticence and the Appeal of Cold Beauty. Reflections on Minimalism', *Funnel*, 1997

'Fosters Brewing Reception Area', *ID Annual Design Review*, no 5, vol 45, 1998, p160

Baik JongWon, 'Case Study: Garry Emery', *DESIGNnet*, no 1998/7, pp44–55

Annemarie Kiely, 'Design Visionaries', *Belle*, no 152, April/May 1999, pp16–48

Joe Rollo, 'Midas Touch', *Monument*, no 30, June/July 1999, p25

Juanita Dugdale, 'Design Down Under', *How*, no 4, July/August 1999, pp40–46

'Pacific Rim Design: Garry Emery', *Quon Editions*, pp136–49

April Greiman, 'Australian Graphic Designers, Emery Vincent Associates, Garry Emery', *Design Exchange*, pp10–15

Honorary positions, Garry Emery

Adjunct Professor, Deakin University, Victoria, Australia

Member of the Alliance Graphique Internationale

Honorary member of the New York Art Directors Club, USA

Member of the New York Type Directors Club, USA

Honorary member of the Tokyo Typo Directors Club, Japan

Honorary member of the International Council of Graphic Design Associations

Honorary member of New Zealand Society of Designers Incorporated

Fellow of the Design Institute of Australia

Lectures by Garry Emery

1988 Key speaker, 'Three approaches to graphic design', The Best, international seminar, New Zealand Society of Designers Incorporated, Auckland, New Zealand

1992 Key speaker, 'Identity through graphic design', design seminar, Singapore Trade Development Board, Singapore

1993 Key speaker, 'Australia: a culture of heterogeneity and paradox', Conferencia International De Diseno Grafico, Ixtapa '93, Mexico

1994 Key speaker, 'International perspective: design and communication after the year 2000', Quality and Context, international seminar, Society of Environmental Graphic Design, Seattle, Washington, USA

1995 Speaker, 'Typography signs and emblems in 2-dimensional and 3-dimensional space', Adobe Expo conference, Melbourne, Australia

1996 Speaker, 'Collaborative balance: beyond the rhetoric', Intersection: the Meeting of Art and Architecture, Royal Australian Institute of Architects national convention, Adelaide, Australia

1999 Key speaker, 'Night cities: international workshop', Massachusetts Institute of Technology, Boston, USA

International design juries, Garry Emery

1992 New York Art Directors Club, New York, USA

1999 Society of Environmental Graphic Design, New York, USA

SELECTED BIBLIOGRAPHY

1992 Gold Award, Tokyo Typo Directors Club, Japan
1994 Gold Award, Biennale of Graphic Design, Brno, Czech Republic
1994 Silver Award, Biennale of Graphic Design, Brno, Czech Republic
1996 Honor Award, Society for Environmental Graphic Design, USA
1996 Two Merit Awards, Society for Environmental Graphic Design, USA
1996 Two Awards for Excellence, New York Type Directors Club, USA
1996 Award for Excellence, Tokyo Typc Directors Club, Japan
1996 Annual Award, Tokyo Typo Directors Club, Japan
1996 Victorian Design Award, Australia
1997 Annual Award, Tokyo Typo Directors Club, Japan
1997 Three Awards of Honour, German Prize for Communications Design, Design Zentrum, Essen, Germany
1997 Good Design Award, The Chicago Athenaeum, Museum of Architecture and Design, USA
1997 Hall of Fame Award, Design Institute of Australia, Australia
1998 Merit Award, Society of Environmental Graphic Design, USA
1998 The President's Award, in recognition of an outstanding contribution to the profession of architecture through the application of specialist skills, Royal Australian Institute of Architects: Victorian chapter, Australia
1998 Design Distinction Award, Annual Design Review, *ID* magazine, USA
1998 Bronze Medal, Poster Biennale, Warsaw, Poland
1998 Award of Excellence *Communication Arts*, USA
1999 Certificate of Typographic Excellence, TDC45, New York Type Directors Club, USA
1999 Gold Medal Award, *Creativity 28*, USA
1999 Tokyo Typo Directors Club Award, Japan
1999 Honourable Mention, ZGRAF8, Zagreb, Croatia
1999 Honorarium, 2nd Internet Graphic Design Competition, Tokyo, Japan

Temporary exhibitions

1991 Seed Hall Seibu Gallery, Tokyo Typo Directors Club, Japan
1992 The Gallery von Oertzen, Frankfurt, Germany
1992 Moravian Gallery, Biennale of Graphic Design, Brno, Czech Republic
1994 Moravian Gallery, Biennale of Graphic Design, Brno, Czech Republic
1994 The 5th International Triennial of Poster Design, Toyama, Japan
1995 Helsinki International Poster Biennale, Helsinki, Finland
1996 The Gallery von Oertzen, Frankfurt, Germany
1997 The 5th International Triennial of Poster Design, Toyama, Japan
1997 Helsinki International Poster Biennale, Helsinki, Finland
1997 International Exhibition, Poster Museum, Lahti, Finland
1997 The Chicago Athenaeum, Museum of Architecture and Design, USA
1998 Moravian Gallery, Biennale of Graphic Design, Brno, Czech Republic

Permanent collections

Museum die Sammlung, Munich Germany
Gotheiner Fine Arts Museum, St Louis, USA
Poster Museum, Wilanow, Poland
Museum für Kunst und Gewerbe, Hamburg, Germany
Mexico City Metropolitan University, Mexico
The Merrill C Berman Collection, New York, USA
The Chicago Athenaeum, Museum of Architecture and Design, USA
Museum of Victoria, Melbourne, Australia
Dansk Plakatmuseum, Abyhoj, Denmark

BIOGRAPHIES

Suzie Attiwill

is a writer and curator.
She collaborated on this book
and also in the preparation
of a major survey exhibition of
the work of Emery Vincent Design
on tour internationally in 2000

Prof Haig Beck

is a Professor in the
Faculty of Architecture at the
University of Melbourne and
editor of UME architectural
magazine. A critic, he has written
in collaboration with
Jackie Cooper on the work of
Emery Vincent Design

Jackie Cooper

is co-editor of UME.
In her capacity as both editor
and copywriter, she has
been closely involved with
Emery Vincent Design for
many years

Dr Peter Steidl

is a corporate identity and
marketing strategist who works
closely with Emery Vincent Design
and collaborates on corporate
identity projects

INDEX